H.D. (Hilda Doolittle)

T0246738

Titles in the series Critical Lives present the work of leading cultural figures of the modern period. Each book explores the life of the artist, writer, philosopher or architect in question and relates it to their major works.

In the same series

H.D. (Hilda Doolittle)

Lara Vetter

REAKTION BOOKS

Published by
REAKTION BOOKS LTD
Unit 32, Waterside
44–48 Wharf Road
London N1 7UX, UK
www.reaktionbooks.co.uk

First published 2023
Copyright © Lara Vetter 2023

Printed and bound in Great Britain by TJ Books Ltd, Padstow, Cornwall

A catalogue record for this book is available from the British Library

ISBN 978 1 78914 759 9

Contents

H.D., early 1920s.

Introduction

This is the story of modernist writer H.D. (Hilda Doolittle), who was written out of literary history before being rediscovered by Susan Stanford Friedman and other scholars in the 1970s and 1980s. Were it not for H.D.'s gender, this erasure would not have occurred. She was, after all, the central figure in the short-lived but profoundly influential Imagist movement, publishing some of the first truly modern free verse in English. Having hatched, with Ezra Pound and Richard Aldington, radical new 'rules' for poetry – an anti-sentimental focus on an image, sparse language, rhythm dictated by content rather than conventional forms – H.D. published three poems in the 1913 issue of *Poetry* that launched a revolution.

Prolific throughout a long career – nearly five decades – she went on to produce not just more and more poetry but autobiographical and historical novels, translations from the ancient Greek, short stories, memoirs, drama, children's literature, reviews and essays on literature and literary history. She also worked in film, as an actor, editor and reviewer. Her career concluded, as did that of many of her modernist poet cohort, with long, ambitious epic poems. She was the first woman to receive the prestigious Award of Merit Medal for Poetry from the American Academy of Arts and Letters.

It may seem surprising that H.D. was born in Pennsylvania, an unlikely incubator for such an innovative writer. But consider this extraordinary convergence of talent: H.D., Marianne Moore, Ezra Pound and William Carlos Williams – four of the most important American poets of the modernist era – were in Philadelphia at the *fin de siècle*. H.D. knew them intimately. Unlike Moore and Williams, H.D. and Pound fled the United States for Europe, arriving wide-eyed at an extraordinary moment in the history of art and literature, an exhilarating time of proliferating manifestos and avant-garde movements: Cubism, Futurism, Dadaism, Surrealism.

H.D. read and wrote about an impressively wide range of topics: gender and sexuality, nature and the environment, religion and mysticism, psychoanalysis, ancient civilizations, the history of war and imperialism, the lives of artists, silent film and literature. She read French, German, Italian, Latin and ancient Greek. She led a fascinating, peripatetic life. At least half a dozen nations she called home: England, the United States, Germany, Greece, Switzerland, Italy. She went to Greece with the sexologist Havelock Ellis. She was in Egypt when King Tutankhamun's tomb was opened. She lived in London through two world wars. Man Ray photographed her twice. Her famed beauty was typically described as strange. She was (quasi-)engaged to Ezra Pound and ended a short-lived friendship with D. H. Lawrence over his sexist views. She was an analysand and patient of Sigmund Freud. Her work ethic could only be described as puritan. She was loyal, at times to a fault. She starred in avant-garde films. She was an amateur astrologer with an expansive, syncretic, ever-evolving, hermetic notion of spirituality. She was extraordinarily well read – her library vast – but in stressful times, she binged on lesbian romances and police procedurals. For a time, she raised pet monkeys.

A fascinating life was a requisite, for H.D. viewed life experience as fodder for her writing. Seducing, being seduced, fuelled her artistic productivity. Deemed the 'perfect-bi' by Freud, she loved men and women. Her romantic relationships were open. She was married but had an extramarital child who was raised by two mothers, and she had four grandchildren. In a time when laws regarding sexual mores were unyielding, she scrupulously guarded her private life, even while her experimental fiction dismantled the line between public and private life, between life and art.

She had a peculiarly modern sense of aesthetics, and a feminist consciousness. She sought always 'a new beauty/ in some terrible/ wind-tortured place'.[1] She was interested in the line between pleasure and pain, and survival in the face of terror. Her earliest verse celebrated the 'slashed and torn' flowers 'with stint of petals . . . thin, sparse of leaf' and decried the manicured roses of a 'sheltered garden'.[2] Her poems resurrected forgotten women and ancient goddesses – Eurydice, Circe, Leda, Simaetha – granting them perspective and voice. She wrote autobiographical fiction that explored her traumas, her desires and the unique struggles of a twentieth-century woman writer. Her novels and epic poems plumbed ancient worlds for insight into contemporary global issues – mapping personal to public trauma. They recount the quests of 'voyagers, discoverers/ of the not-known', who recover cultural memory.[3] Inscribed on her tombstone in Bethlehem, Pennsylvania, her epitaph remembers H.D. as 'one who died/ following intricate song's/ lost measure'.[4]

H.D. rarely smiled for photographs. In the early days of the medium, of course, photographs were largely staged, not candid snapshots. Having portraits made, whether painted or shot by a camera, were momentous occasions. But H.D.'s photographs were particularly theatrical. A woman writer in a time when women's writing was so often dismissed, her images convey gravitas. Her gaze so often just misses us, as if she is studiously examining an object of grand importance that is just out of view. Even photographs that were not commissioned – for public distribution, or to accompany published work – are imbued with intensity and beauty, but never frivolity. Pictures of her touring through Greece and Egypt look more like fashion shoots than holiday photos. Snapshots with her daughter and grandchildren show ferocity and focus.

As Sarah Parker and Jade French argue, photography 'was central to H.D's self-fashioning'.[5] Their recent article does a lovely job surveying many of the photographic portraits we have of her. As a woman writer, H.D. was ever conscious of the fine line between good publicity and bad, between an image that might be productively self-promotional and one that would serve merely to objectify her and diminish her work. She vamps, she poses, she performs, but in the end her photographic image must reflect seriousness and dedication to craft.

At every stage – from her childhood to her old age – photographs of H.D. are more in line with her work than with her life. She guarded her private life as rigorously as she did her image, and she shrewdly cultivated her public persona. It is not lost on me that I have spent a great deal of time and energy on a biographical project that, almost certainly, H.D. herself would never have approved. It is not, I think, that there are facts revealed here that she would have wished suppressed. She adapted to changing mores throughout her life, and I have little doubt that she would have embraced the flexible conceptions of gender and sexuality that we have come to take for granted today. But she would have balked at giving over control of her story. Her prose fiction articulates a powerfully nuanced sense of the politics of narrative. She nurtured a distrust of academics, and she loathed the biographies of her modernist comrades that had begun to appear in the final decade of her life, even as she devoured them.

H.D. was incredibly ambitious – difficult then, difficult even now for women. She did not at all mind that early reviewers and readers of her verse could not discern her gender. It is true that she detested her birth name – Doolittle bespoke idleness and disempowerment – but she also had no wish to disclose her gender, her marital status or her nationality. Once her reputation was established, she minded less the circulation of her image, but she remained steadfast in concealing biographical details, wishing the work to stand on its own. Those who violated those restrictions – such as the poet Amy Lowell, who once tricked H.D.'s mother into revealing details about her daughter – slipped, gradually, from her orbit. While she was well aware of the pitfalls of being typecast as 'H.D., *Imagiste*', she learned quickly how to use the power of that signature – and the expectations it generated – to further her work. She expertly nudged the boundaries of 'H.D.'-ness, probing its vulnerabilities, as her verse shifted away from Imagist principles and towards more lengthy, dynamic epic forms.

Her efforts, we would agree today, were successful. Though she was written out of literary history following her death in 1961, she left copious breadcrumbs for us to follow. She was keenly aware that what her literary executor, Norman Holmes Pearson, termed her 'shelf' at the Beinecke Library at Yale University would cement her legacy. She was, increasingly as she aged, supremely confident that she was ahead of her time. She rightly surmised that what publishers in her time refused to print – manuscripts they either didn't understand or deemed not worthy of 'H.D.' – would be lauded by a later generation. She is read and studied widely now as one of a small group of high modernists who challenged the literary conventions of the day, offering a new aesthetic and a new framework for seeing the world.

What is extraordinary about H.D., however, is that at the same time as she safeguarded her private life – maintaining so rigidly the line between private and public – she also worked to deconstruct this divide, in a time before 'deconstruct' was a verb in common parlance. Indeed, she barely conceded that there was a divide at all. Work, for H.D., was the material and aesthetic embodiment of experience, of a life lived. Her life, her body, was a canvas. Work did not reflect life. Rather, she wrote her life into existence. She was ever mindful that it is narratives that construct identity, and not the other way around. For much of her adult life she migrated between spheres of living and spheres of writing. Throwing herself into the nightlife of vibrant cities, into gossip, into romantic liaisons with men and women, into museums and ancient ruins, she would then escape to quieter, usually rural or isolated locales at which she could dedicate herself to prose, poetry and translations inspired by her experiences. More than once she compared a writer to a scientist: 'Fling acid, base into a crystal test tube . . . watch and watch things sizzle'.[6]

In a remarkable seven-hundred-page tribute to her work, the contemporary poet Robert Duncan observed: 'Life, itself, it seemed always to H.D. was "like a work of art" or was "a work of art" – a poetry. What is important here is that she took whatever she could, whatever hint of person or design, color or line, over into her "work."'[7] Perhaps this is why H.D., who shielded herself meticulously from public scrutiny, nonetheless employed the autobiographical mode to a greater extent than most if not all of her modernist cohort. She wrote repeatedly about the most traumatic and private parts of her life: her childhood, her sexuality, her stillbirth, her infidelity and that of her husband, her day-to-day existence.

She lived – I have become more and more certain – to write. When Pearson made it clear that strategic self-disclosure would ensure her canonization, she eagerly penned several memoirs in her final two decades. But I do not mean to suggest that she was a heartless mercenary. H.D. enjoyed, as I hope I have shown in what follows, a rich interior and emotional existence. She immersed herself in life experience with abandon, sought out and submitted herself not only to love and joy but to sadness and pain. She was, by all accounts, unusually sensitive; she felt adversity more deeply than most. Yet she did not shy away from difficulties or challenges.

She championed the survival instincts of the meek and the frail. She transformed trauma into art. As one of her lovers, Silvia Dobson, told another, Bryher, 'Here was a precious yet vulnerable person, too delicate for exposure to the elements, yet determined to be extravagantly exposed.'[8]

Such a figure – who at once upheld and dismantled the line between interiority and exteriority, one who curated her image and reputation – poses not insignificant challenges to a biographer. On what evidence can a biographer of H.D. draw? The corpus of imaginative writing, and the copious letters she wrote daily, each crafted with a particular recipient in mind. We have, too, the work and letters of others, which stem from their own limitations, inspirations, motives and motivations. And we don't have it all. H.D. spent years selecting what made it onto her shelf at Yale. Much was destroyed. This is an unavoidable problem for all biographers – archives, as Ann Laura Stoler has argued, are not 'sites of knowledge retrieval but of knowledge production'[9] – but a biographer of H.D. must proceed cautiously, aware that H.D. (and her lifelong partner Bryher) quite consciously bequeathed an obstacle course for a biographer to navigate.

There are other unavoidable issues at stake for any biographer: as Diane Middlebrook, Anne Sexton's biographer, observes, 'neither author nor subject in a biography is uninfluenced by points of view that structure the cultures that fostered them.'[10] A biographer in the early 1980s simply did not have, for instance, precisely the same conceptions of gender and sexuality that we have four decades later. A biography written forty years hence will have yet a different notion of how to navigate H.D.'s complicated sexualities.

How, moreover, does a biographer weave the work of the writer smoothly into an account of her life without constantly creating tenuous connections between one and the other? This is particularly a problem, I quickly learned, with a *short* biography of the life and the work of a writer who lived as long and wrote as much as H.D. I have much sympathy for Llewellin Jegels when he writes that he felt 'a sharp pang of guilt' whenever he had to leave out some aspect of his subject's life narrative.[11] It is no exaggeration to say that I had to leave out far more than I included here. But omission is inevitable. As H.D. herself wrote in a fictionalization of her own life, 'I could more or less tell it in a paragraph. I could spend my life on ten long volumes and just begin to get the skeleton framework of it.'[12]

Another challenge is that accounts of H.D.'s demeanour and personality swing wildly between poles. At various points in her life, with various people, in various contexts, you will find a different H.D. She is tomboyish, assertive, confident, reclusive, shy and fearful. She is mercurial. She is detached and aloof, a loner. She is quiet and sensitive. She is flamboyant, witty and seductive. She is painfully vulnerable, always hiding from view. She is glamorous and charming, inviting attention. She shies away from social settings, stooping to minimize her presence and extravagant height (she is nearly six feet tall). She is a skilled conversationalist. She is gangly, fragile and physically awkward. She is an athlete, excelling at basketball and tennis. She has many friends and lovers. She is private. Her attention ever drifts into an otherworldly space, away from the quotidian. She craves gossip. She is fierce, committed slavishly to her craft, a bit anal-retentive, unbending in routine, intolerant of noise. She loves to listen to loud music. She is always serious. She is funny, 'saltily American, humorous, informal'.[13] She had a laugh 'like a waterfall, or a tinkling cascade of bells'.[14] She had a wicked sense of humour and a sharp wit, her daughter recalled.

Her friend James Whitall admitted, 'H.D. is an intensely difficult personality to describe.'[15] Her first love, Frances Gregg, simply embraced the contradictions: 'Hilda was entrancing. Hilda was ridiculous. Hilda was exquisite. Hilda was hideous.'[16] This is, of course, a problem for every biographer. Humans are not the same from birth to death. We evolve, we develop, we change. We also craft different versions of ourselves for different people in our lives. But in the case of H.D., her portrayal of herself in autobiographical novels and short stories is radically inconsistent. Different autobiographical texts covering the same periods of her life diverge not just in style but in content. A character who is central to one narrative does not appear in the others. Characters across texts based on the same real-life person are portrayed so differently as to be unrecognizable. Scenes key to one text are missing in others. The First World War looms over some of her accounts of the 1910s but is scarcely mentioned elsewhere. H.D.'s autobiographically based persona is a lesbian in one, bisexual in two, heterosexual in another. Marital infidelity is a major theme of two of these volumes, but others focus instead on coming into one's own as a woman writer.

What is a biographer to make of such dramatic disregard for consistency? And if after so many attempts to capture her 'self' in prose even H.D. was unable to do so, how can a biographer succeed where she failed? We must, it is obvious, reframe the questions. H.D. did not, by the end of her career, quite believe in the metaphysical entity of the 'self'. Probably she never had. A 'loss of identity', she writes in 'Narthex', is a 'gift'.[17] She seems aware, from an early point in her career, that she writes the self into existence. Even her earliest autobiographical effort foregrounds self as construction. In *Paint It Today* the unnamed narrator – 'a nebulous personality without a name' – takes pains to distance herself from her autobiographically based protagonist, Midget, 'the person (who was, more or less, myself)'.[18] She expresses uncertainty in her protagonist's innermost thoughts, and struggles with her for narrative control. H.D. was well aware in her autobiographical endeavours that she wasn't just creating the story but that 'the story must create me.'[19] What is more, H.D. was not herself unaware of the challenges of biography, having written one of Elizabeth Siddall in the late 1940s. *White Rose and the Red* is a narrative as much about narratives regarding Siddall as it is a narrative of Siddall. Of her subject, H.D. remarks pointedly: 'Her humanity was at war with the fiction woven round her.'[20] I suspect she often thought the same of herself.

I embarked on this project with a naive commitment to avoiding the trap of writing a coherent, cohesive life. I wished to offer some sense of 'who she was' – biographies require 'a person, a consistently represented self at the center of the book'[21] – while, at the same time, avoiding a totalizing portrait that ignores the inconsistencies that we, as humans, all have. But I have been humbled by the process. Teleology is seductive. The temptation to theorize, to assert causal links, to produce a meta-narrative to explain a life, is impossible to resist entirely. A biography that does not tell a story, that simply casts out a series of facts or a timeline or omits the invisible, psychological layer of human existence, is a biography few would wish to read. And yet narrative, as Hayden White and countless others – even H.D. herself – have reminded us, is based in the principles of fiction. Biographical narrative comes with the expectations we have of any narrative: consistent, believable characters who undergo change; a story arc; an ending that ties up loose ends. My subjects became characters. I had to plot it all out, to storyboard it. Strict adherence to chronology was impossible if the story was to be understood by readers. At times, I have had to rely on H.D.'s own autobiographical accounts, but I have been careful to cite and contextualize them as such, particularly in cases in which there is no corroborating evidence. As I teetered towards fiction, I feared that accuracy flagged.

I have also had to navigate how to handle the name of my subject. The intricacies of H.D.'s tenuous notion of the 'self' extended even to how she referred to herself. In private life, she was Hilda Aldington; she hated her given surname. But H.D. viewed 'H.D.' as a particular persona, a writer of poetry and of writing about poetry (usually, though not exclusively). Her fictional, non-fictional and film pursuits were often the product of other personae: Helga Dart, Sylvania Penn, Rhoda Peter, Helga Doorn, J. Beran, Edith Gray, John Helforth, Delia Alton. Since her death, however, we have published her work with the initials H.D. In this book, she is Hilda until she publishes her first poems in *Poetry* in 1913; thereafter she is H.D. Though she had signed her name 'H.D.' before that point – stories of Pound christening her with that moniker are apocryphal – it is the author 'H.D.' who is born in that moment.

There is theory, and there is praxis. This couldn't be an innovative postmodern biography, for she is not a figure well known enough to carry that burden. The book, too, is meant to be a short introduction of the life and work of H.D., not comprehensive or critical. As such it requires a certain coherence. Its primary audience is broad, not just scholars but general readers. I broke the life and work up into seven phases. Chapters are organized by spans of years. Within each, chronology loosens, the focus, rather, on particular personages, key events and prominent themes that dominate the period.

I drafted this text during the bizarre isolation of the COVID-19 pandemic. I wrote drawing entirely on her work and on archival materials collected and notes taken over the past two and a half decades, with occasional forays into scholarship on H.D.'s work that I admire. (It would be two years before the Beinecke Rare Book and Manuscript Library would reopen and I would be able to supplement my prior notes, confirm claims and dates, and so on.) I consulted the invaluable 'Silverstein Chronology' – painstakingly compiled by an intrepid Yale University librarian – always checking it against my own research.

I did not reread Barbara Guest's 1984 biography before or during the process. I completed the book before two new biographies appeared. I did not make this decision because other biographies don't have merit. The community of H.D. scholars is, and has always been, extraordinarily generous and accomplished, and their work has been invaluable to shaping my sense of her. But, for this volume, I wished to let her creative work and the archival evidence speak to me without the frameworks of other biographical endeavours. An impossibility? Absolutely. A worthwhile pursuit? Yes, I think so. I cannot un-read what I have read – or un-know what I have known – but I did assay to read her work and my notes anew. Particular themes emerged from this process – some familiar to me, some surprising – that offer threads for readers to follow: H.D.'s ambition and impressive work ethic, her capacious sense of sexuality and gender, her equally capacious spiritual and metaphysical views, her belief that life is fodder for art.

Written under these conditions, this volume represents *my* H.D. We do not have the luxury, thankfully, in the 2020s of believing that every biography does not bear the undeniable imprint of its author. At a final stage, I glanced back at Guest's biography and other biographical sources and eagerly perused new books by Susan McCabe and Donna Krolik Hollenberg, adding a citation or two where appropriate. My hope is that readers will be inspired by my book to read more by and about a figure who has held my fascination for over three decades. Our experience can only be enriched by reading multiple accounts of H.D.'s life. As H.D. once explained to her young daughter, Perdita, 'My past, the past, the past that never was, and making something real of it . . . it's always eluding me. I think I've found it, and I find it's wrong. But the wrong way can be illuminating too.'[22]

There is one photograph of H.D. to which I keep returning. In this photograph, she smiles directly into the camera lens, unabashedly

Hilda, 1902 or 1903.

joyful, her eyes sparkling mischievously. It is a candid shot of a young H.D. in rural Pennsylvania, at the *fin de siècle* – Hilda in an unguarded moment. Her happiness is palpable. She is outdoors, amidst the flora that would fill so much verse to come. Sunlight dapples half of her face and blurs part of the picture, imparting otherworldly streaks of light and shadow. Victorian garb was still the norm, and she would not shed it entirely for well over a decade. But here her long skirt is flowing, loose, informal. We have caught her in the act of climbing – yes, climbing – over a fence in a skirt, blissfully careless of sullying her dress. She has yet to move to Europe. She has yet to become a well-known writer. I like to imagine that this photograph is evidence that, despite (or because of) her frustrations with the insularity of the family home, she is already determined to live an adventurous, audacious life, a life of rebellion, against the currents that channel a woman's life into constricted rivulets and streams. I like to imagine that this is a moment when H.D. dwells, as Emily Dickinson wrote, in possibility.

1

'inexorably entangled', 1886–1911

At the opening of one of H.D.'s many autobiographical novels, *HERmione*, her titular protagonist receives two letters: one from a male suitor, a budding poet, George; the other an invitation to meet an alluring young female art student, Fayne, who by the end of the novel will provoke the realization that Hermione was among those 'people who loved . . . differently'.[1] The two will be magnets that attract her in opposite directions – aesthetically and erotically. But here, at the beginning of the book, Hermione is already at a crossroads. She suffers from an 'entire failure to conform'.[2] A short-lived stint at college was a disaster, but she hasn't yet grasped that she perceives the world through the eyes of an artist, not a scholar. She may or may not wish to marry George. Life in Pennsylvania is suffocating; she wants the sting of the salt of the sea, not the tightening canopy of inland trees. She feels longing, but does not yet comprehend what it is she desires. She feels herself 'clutch toward something that had no name yet'.[3]

It is, perhaps, not surprising that in *HERmione* H.D. describes being 'shut in a little box',[4] for she had been reared in an unusually insular community. On 10 September 1886, Hilda Doolittle was born in Bethlehem, Pennsylvania, to Charles and Helen Doolittle. Bethlehem had been founded in 1741, 80 kilometres (50 mi.) north of Philadelphia, when the wealthy Philadelphia businessman William Allen gifted 200 hectares (500 ac) of land to the Moravian Church, land that had been part of the Lenape Nation. It was a

Hilda, 1880s.

beautiful, wooded site perched on the banks of the Lehigh River. In the 1800s it was still quite small, with only 5,000–6,000 residents. Helen Wolle Doolittle's family had lived there since the eighteenth century, when Matthias Weiss immigrated from Germany in 1743. The colonial-era Moravians lived communally, earning no wages and relying on the Church to provide for them. As the Moravians were a deeply evangelical sect, Bethlehem was but one of many settlements across the world, in regions as far flung as the Virgin Islands, Greenland and present-day South Africa.

By 1886, the town was home to Lehigh University, where Charles Leander Doolittle was professor of mathematics and astronomy,

Charles Leander Doolittle with telescope.

and a burgeoning steel mill industry. Bethlehem Steel was for a time the second-largest steel producer in the United States, and the hulky steelworks towered along the river shore. Hilda's family lived in Old Town, on Church Street, next door to her maternal grandparents, Elizabeth Weiss Wolle and the Reverend Francis Wolle, past principal of the Moravian Ladies Seminary, clergyman and a botanist specializing in algae. Hilda and her parents shared their home with her three brothers and two half-brothers – a sister, Edith, had died in 1883 after only five months of life. Aunts, uncles and a bevy of cousins lived nearby. 'The town contains scarcely anyone who is not a relative or friend,' she would recall years later.[5] Charles dropped out of college to volunteer for the Union Army as a private in the Civil War when he was only seventeen, then completed his education at the University of Michigan before accepting a position at Lehigh in 1875.[6] He was also an occasional versifier.[7] His first wife, Martha Farrand, died in his first year in Bethlehem. When he began courting Helen, a musician and painter, she told him that she wasn't interested in marrying a widower. She swiftly changed her mind, however, when she learned that her father intended to marry her to a missionary posted in St Thomas, in the Caribbean. She and Charles wed in 1883.

As an astronomer, Charles often worked at night, so he built a study with sleeping accommodations, set apart from what was surely a raucous household. The scent of leather books filled his office, a pleasant aroma that mingled with the smell emanating from the porcelain wood stove that warmed the room.[8] Ornamenting his office were scores of pens and ink bottles, a stuffed white owl, jars and pots and bottles, a skull and a magnifying glass that could be spirited away to set fires.[9] Hilda deemed it a privilege when she was permitted to quietly play there.

As 'house-daughter' – the only daughter in the family – it was her duty to help her mother run the household.[10] Her chores done, the tomboyish Hilda could usually be found scampering

Helen Wolle Doolittle at the easel.

about outdoors with her brothers, cousins and friends, amidst the gardens that first inspired her love of flowers, the lush pear and crab apple trees that flourished in their neighbourhood and the grape arbour the children loved to climbed. Hilda was particularly close to her half-brother Eric, who, following in his father's footsteps, taught astronomy at Lehigh and occasionally tutored her and the other children. Eric's lessons in ecology unveiled to the children a fantastical world of teeming insects and undergrowth that rendered Hilda 'spellbound'. 'There were things under things, as well as things inside things,' she rhapsodized.[11] Some days their grandmother took the children to play in the nearby cemetery, showering them with lime drops and mint cakes if they were well behaved.

Hilda's Uncle Hartley kept a live alligator as a pet, and the children fed it raw meat through the wire mesh of its cage. Its escape – a fall from the attic window – created quite a stir, but otherwise, Hilda's early life was uneventful and highly ritualized: certain foods were only made on certain days; the women of the community did the washing and the baking at the same time. Charles was quiet, even-tempered and largely absent, while Helen, already kept busy managing the lively household, taught music and painting, and participated in the religious community that enveloped them. The Moravian religious rituals – love feasts, Easter week festivities, vespers, church picnics, midnight service at New Year's Eve – offered the youth delicious treats and a strong sense of belonging. Children were integrated into religious functions, carrying beeswax candles home from chapel, singing in the choir and aiding the adults in constructing elaborate 'putzes' (or nativity scenes) at Christmas time.

Theirs was a tight-knit religious community. The older members of the church still spoke German, and the Moravian Parochial School was sex-segregated. As Hilda's cousin Francis put it in his memoir, 'we children were shaped by the Christian religion as exemplified in the Moravian Church, by a strong family tradition based on devotion to that church, and by the host of relatives who surrounded us and cared about our welfare. The conditions seemed almost idyllic.'[12] Music filled the church, and the house: it was important to Moravians, and many of Hilda's relatives were talented musicians, including her great-great-grandfather Peter Wolle, who created the Moravian hymnbook, and her uncle J. Fred Wolle, who is today credited with popularizing Bach for American audiences. Hilda, then, not surprisingly, was a skilled pianist at a young age. Looking back, H.D. would note what a strange, narrow life she had as a child – though not an unhappy one.

When Hilda was eight, however, everything changed when her father took a position at the University of Pennsylvania, running the Flower Observatory in an exurb of Philadelphia called Upper Darby. The family moved to a large three-storey brick-and-stone house, which rested on the observatory's 3-hectare (7 ac) plot, and, with no Moravian church nearby, they became Quakers. The extroverted Hilda became shy and reserved, the abrupt move causing 'a complete psychic break with my little friends and life and school – a great shock in some way to me, that drove me inward, introverted me'.[13] Her anxiety was no doubt exacerbated by an incident that occurred not long after the move: Charles suffered a concussion in a tram accident, which traumatized Hilda and the other children, who tended to their father until their mother got home. In later years, Hilda would return to this incident time and time again.

It took some time to adjust to living far from the close-knit community of Moravian Pennsylvania. But proximity to Philadelphia brought new pleasures, and she would eventually remember her early years in Upper Darby as 'a return to happy childhood'.[14] Though they were closer to a big city, the new location was truly rural – the population was around 3,000 – situated at least a mile away from the closest village. The children took full advantage of the expansive garden, the woods surrounding them and the numerous creeks that adorned the landscape, but an interest in drama was developing, too, as Hilda and her brothers matured. She began attending plays and appearing in them at school. At home, Hilda and her brother Gilbert, along with her new

Hilda, high-school graduation photo, 1905.

schoolfriend Reneé Athené, performed musicals and Shakespeare plays.[15] Hilda revelled in the cross-dressing roles, adopting the headstrong Rosalind of *As You Like It* as her favourite character.[16] The family vacationed along the 'lovely wild water-ways' of the northeastern shore, from New Jersey to Rhode Island to Maine, nurturing a deep love of the sea.[17]

Initially Hilda attended Miss Gordon's School for Girls, taking the trolley into the city each day. Founded in 1880, the institution focused on teaching girls French, music and college preparatory skills, and it was there that Hilda met Margaret Snively – who would become a lifelong friend – and other girls destined, as was she, for

Bryn Mawr. At Miss Gordon's, her teacher recognized her talent for literature, even as she chastised Hilda for her love of Edgar Allan Poe.[18] In 1902, Hilda, like many of Miss Gordon's girls, graduated and went on to Friends Central preparatory school, where she took Latin and ancient Greek history while preparing for the infamously difficult Bryn Mawr entrance exams. At her commencement ceremony in 1905, she was invited to read an original essay with a title, 'The Poet's Influence', that hinted at her fate.[19]

Hilda, early 1900s.

Hilda, 1901.

A few years earlier, at the age of fifteen, Hilda had briefly met the poet Ezra Pound, Gilbert's classmate at the University of Pennsylvania, at a Halloween party to which he wore a memorable green 'Indo-China-ish' robe.[20] Ezra transferred to Hamilton College, and when he returned, the year she graduated from high school, the two reconnected. They were fervently interested in literature, art and religion, and they conducted a romantic friendship for several years. He called her 'Dryad'. While Hilda is often portrayed as Ezra's muse and protégé, her knowledge of ancient Greece and the Greek language was in fact far superior to his at this point. Indeed,

Ezra – otherwise a polyglot – found ancient Greek so difficult that he customized his own plan of study in college to avoid taking it.[21]

Ezra Loomis Pound was born in Idaho to Homer and Isabel Pound, but his mother moved him to the east coast within six months of his birth, and the family were settled just north of Philadelphia by the time Hilda's family moved to Upper Darby. Ezra was a year older than she, flamboyant and manic, striking rather than handsome, with blue eyes and a bushy mass of red hair. Her autobiographical novel *Paint It Today* describes him as 'a hectic, adolescent, blundering, untried, mischievous, and irreverent male youth'.[22] In *End to Torment*, she remembers him as 'immensely sophisticated, immensely superior, immensely rough-and-ready, a product not like any of the brothers and brothers' friends'.[23] He made himself conspicuous. The poet John Gould Fletcher found him always fashionably, if idiosyncratically, attired, energetic and 'pugnacious', but with a surprisingly 'high-pitched, shrill, almost feminine voice'.[24] Ezra and Hilda read to each other in her brother's treehouse and attended school dances – he danced poorly. They shared a love for hazelnut chocolates, took long walks together in the woods and shared kisses 'electric, magnetic'.[25] He wrote poems to her, compiling them in a parchment folder entitled 'Hilda's Book'. A pearl engagement ring was bestowed, then returned a couple of months later. Charles and Helen burned his letters to Hilda,[26] and forbade their marriage after a scandal at Wabash College, where he was teaching Romance languages before a night spent with a young, unmarried woman resulted in his dismissal.

Hilda studied the classics at Bryn Mawr, where she met her lifelong friend Marianne Moore, the poet. But, unlike Moore, she did not finish her degree. Her parents had been hopeful that she would study science, like her father, but her passions lay elsewhere; she was also undoubtedly hampered by their decision to keep her at home while other girls lived in the dorms. She sought out companions who shared her interests, maintaining an expansive friend group that included Ezra, Margaret and her brother DeForest Snively, Louise Skidmore (with whom Hilda vacationed on Long Island), the poet William Carlos Williams, the painter William Brooke Smith and Mary and Bob Lamberton, as well as a string of college friends. They spent time picnicking along streams and millponds; attending performances; throwing teas, coasting socials, and Halloween parties; and vacationing with each other's families. Hilda seemed as happy frolicking in the ocean or woods as she was hosting parties. She was, as Helen Carr notes, 'totally undomesticated; she liked to rush round the countryside, her clothes thrown on anyhow, her hair wild.'[27] Williams recounted fondly an afternoon with her: 'We talked of the finest things: of Shakespeare, of flowers, trees, books, & pictures and meanwhile climbed fences and walked through woods and climbed little hills till it began to grow just dusky when we arrived at our destination.'[28] The group relished the freedom of the Snively household when Margaret's parents were away, though on one such evening, Hilda was mortified to discover that her friends had spied on her and Ezra kissing.

By the time Ezra sailed to Europe in 1908, Hilda, at the age of 21, had become determined to move to Europe herself. She wanted to be a writer and saw no path to that goal in Philadelphia, and though she was hardly suited for a domestic occupation, she was even willing to consider a position as an au pair, or to 'scrub floors to get abroad'.[29] After leaving Bryn Mawr midway through her second year she taught piano, and briefly enrolled in a college course for teachers at the University of Pennsylvania, but she longed to write. She had begun to act informally as a poetry editor, probably for Ezra, though she offered her services to Williams as well: 'if you want me to make scathing remarks about diction, rhyme scheme, connotation, denotation, etc., just ship down your literature.'[30] (Williams must have respected her literary judgement because he responded with a poem.)

Hilda's first kiss with Ezra may have been 'electric', but it paled in comparison to her first meeting with Frances Josepha Gregg, a scholarship student at the Pennsylvania Academy of the Fine Arts. Gregg lived with her mother, Julia, in northwest Philadelphia. Julia worked as a public-school teacher at the Washington Combined Primary School on Carpenter Street, and the two lived modestly. Julia Gregg started the first school for Italian immigrants and became an activist for their rights.[31] Frances's father was Oliver Howard Gregg, but she did not grow up with him. Julia claimed to be a widow and called herself Julia Vanness Gregg, though she was born, in New Orleans, Julia Maria Lang. Julia was a lesbian.

In a fictionalized account in *Paint It Today*, H.D. employs religious language to capture the breathtaking impact of meeting Frances for the first time, comparing it to the divine light that came to Paul on the road to Damascus when Jesus spoke to him. When she first glimpsed Frances, she felt 'the floor sink beneath her feet and the wall rise to infinity above her head'.[32] Frances's eyes were 'an unholy splendor', 'the blue eyes it is said one sees in heaven', 'eyes the color of wet hyacinths before the spikes have broken into flower'. She 'devour[ed] like a storm that space of uttermost and bluest heaven'.[33] Hilda found eyes endlessly alluring and had been disappointed in Ezra's, 'his least impressive feature'.[34] She would spend her life seeking lovers whose eyes resembled Gregg's.

Hilda was entranced, and she and Frances became very close, spending intimate nights together at the Doolittle home. The two read poetry together, basking in suggestive lines of Decadent verse. As Cassandra Laity has argued, H.D. found in Swinburne conceptions of androgyny and homoeroticism that would excite and inspire her, a model for a 'homoerotic bond with a "sister" muse', and a vehicle through which women could 'extricate themselves from the strict sex-gender codes that polarize the sexes'.[35] If Ezra had shown her 'what love might be or become if one, in desperation, should accept the shadow of an understanding for an understanding itself', H.D. wrote in *Paint It Today*, then Frances taught her 'what love was or could be or become if the earth . . . should be swept from beneath our feet, and we were left ungravitated between the stars'.[36]

Frances held progressive beliefs about sexuality. Like Hilda, she was bisexual and polyamorous, viewing both gender and sexuality as non-binary: 'Male and femaleness in sexual matters is remarkably inconclusive and fluid,' she opined: 'male and female characteristics weave and intertwine.'[37] A concerned Ezra warned them that they would have been burned at the stake as witches had they lived in Salem a century previous.[38] After meeting the 'cacophonic calamity' that was Ezra, Frances pursued both of them successfully, creating a romantic triangle – a pattern that would recur in Hilda's future relationships.[39]

Frances's response to Hilda was more measured than Hilda's to her, but there is no doubt that she, too, was profoundly affected by the relationship, if a little frightened of Hilda's intensity.[40] Frances was volatile and could be mean-spirited – later her lover John Cowper Powys referred to her as his 'Sadista'.[41] At a particularly low point, H.D. saved Frances from a half-hearted suicide attempt, but the experience only served to deepen their connection: finding her in a stream, 'Hilda undressed me herself, and oh her hands were swift and gentle. She warmed my hands against her breast and called them her birds, and made crooning, soft, witless talk that eased my childish, overcharged heart.'[42] Like Hilda, Frances was relatively inexperienced, though she had had a romantic friendship with a young woman named Amy Hoyt, with whom she worked at the Young Ladies' Auxiliary of the Presbyterian Home for Widows and Single Women. Looking back in her memoir *The Mystic Leeway*, she recalled of Hilda, 'I brooded and brooded upon that face, reading it and re-reading it, like a thrilling, endless book.'[43] Their erotic connection fuelled and channelled Hilda's incipient desire to

Frances Josepha Gregg.

be a writer: 'you draw things out of me,' she tells Fayne in *HERmione*. 'Love is writing,' she declares emphatically, defying George's edict that 'love doesn't make good art.'[44] Indeed, though she had done a few verse translations at school, H.D. wrote her very first original poems for Frances in free verse, modelled on the homoerotic idylls of Theocritus.

By 1910, Hilda had begun to feel frustrated living with her parents, who, she suspected, were disappointed in her when she left Bryn Mawr.[45] Her family home felt increasingly stifling, an environment decidedly unsuited to literary pursuits. In October of that year, at Ezra's urging and with her father's financial assistance, she moved to New York City, about a mile from Ezra, at Patchin Place in the Village – lodgings that went on to attract a literary crowd, including both Djuna Barnes and e. e. cummings. She shared the flat with Julia Wells, a friend of Ezra's and the sister of one of Hilda's classmates from Miss Gordon's.[46] Hilda was miserable there, and the experiment lasted only about five months. She was scandalized by her 'sordid' surroundings, an indication of the extent to which she had been sheltered and closely monitored by her family.[47]

Still, if she was not yet making a living at it, she had become a professional writer by 1909, taking advantage of one of the only markets for women's writing in that period: the romance genre. A school friend, Mary Marshall Duffee, was writing an advice column for the McClure syndicate, one of the first successful literary syndicates in the United States. This was just the connection Hilda needed to launch her career. Under the pseudonym Edith Gray (the first name taken from her lost sister), Hilda authored at least eight short romance stories, which appeared in wide circulation in both small-town and big-city newspapers – from the *Elmore County Republican* in Idaho and the *Checotah Times* in Oklahoma to the *Boston Globe* – between 1909 and 1911. Some stories are quite traditional, ending in marriage or portraying the reunion of lost loves, but others push back on gender norms. In one, a woman writer delights in telling stories of romance but has no interest in cultivating one of her own. In another, a woman waits to seek a life partner only after she has enjoyed professional success as a writer. In several stories, she documents how women are driven by societal forces into loveless marriages.

The syndicate did not pay well, but religious newspapers did. Using Homer Pound's contacts with local Presbyterian newspapers, 'Edith Gray' began writing short stories for children and young adults, which appeared between 1910 and 1913. Most of these stories were for and about young children, typically featuring an imaginative, mischievous boy who seeks out adventures that often involve talking animals or other supernatural personages who function to lead him back to the comforts of home. Intended for publication in religious serials, they bear a moral lesson. Young David, for instance, learns to take better care of his little sister, or to do better in school. She penned three stories about life in girls' boarding schools, though only one of these was published, the other two undoubtedly too edgy in their accounts of a teacher–schoolgirl elopement and lesbian attraction.

The later stories, published in 1912 and 1913, show real growth as a writer. But Hilda had no intention of building a career on what her mother, in *HERmione*, termed 'dear little stories'.[48] To be an artist, she needed to put more distance between herself and her family, and between herself and the United States, known even then as an industrial and technological giant, not a centre of the arts. Hilda Doolittle was going to Europe.

2

'my pencil run riot!', 1911–14

Let us imagine the world of European art that Hilda Doolittle would jubilantly encounter in the summer of 1911. Cubism debuted in Paris that year, in a group show at the 'Salon des Indépendants' exhibition that featured work by such groundbreaking painters as Fernand Léger and Robert Delaunay. The fervour of the public outcry – and the vitriol of the critics – in response to this introduction to the art of the future surprised even the participating artists. In Italy, F. T. Marinetti published his Futurist manifesto, promoting kinetic art that extolled technology, masculinity and youth, and declaring war 'one form of hygiene for the world'.[1] 'With us begins the reign of the man whose roots are cut, the multiplied man who merges himself with iron, is fed by electricity, and no longer understands anything except the sensual delight of danger and quotidian heroism,' Marinetti exclaimed.[2] In Germany, Kandinsky's revolt against art took the form of Der Blaue Reiter, a precursor to Expressionism that emphasized painting as a vehicle for spiritual truths, and in England, Wyndham Lewis and the Post-impressionists of the Camden Town Group rendered bleak, quotidian urban settings and garishly tinted portraits. It was an era of proliferating avant-garde movements and manifestos.

It is impossible to overstate the intensity of Hilda's feelings upon finally leaving the United States for France and England. Nearly two decades later, it remained, as she put it simply, her 'happiest moment'.[3] In late July of 1911, at a New York City port, Hilda,

Frances Gregg and Frances's mother, Julia, bid farewell to William Carlos Williams and Hilda's father as they set sail for France on ss *Floride*, a French freighter that Hilda called her 'Argo'.[4] The term recalls the ancient Greek story of Jason's quest for the golden fleece that held the key to his royal ascension, and thus suggests the power she believed to be awaiting her in Europe, and the extent of her unquenchable ambition. In *The Mystic Leeway*, Gregg recollects: 'We were dizzy, drunk, with excitement . . . It was a unique, an impossible, and an incredible adventure.'[5]

The level of excitement must have been high indeed, given that their trip took place in the midst of one of the worst heatwaves in European history; over 40,000 people died in France alone between July and September. Aside from Frances's brief phrase 'the hot summer of 1911', and Hilda's 'very hot', the extreme conditions bear no mention in their renditions of that trip – their memories flooded instead with the novelty of the European experience.[6] Gregg did recall the modest conditions of the ship, an episode of food poisoning and a lack of privacy, as well as a particularly traumatic moment in which they watched a man fall overboard to his death. The crossing itself was turbulent, but none of this detracted from their shared sense of anticipation. When she wasn't quarrelling with Frances's overbearing mother – spats about Hilda's corruption of Frances's innocence persisted throughout their trip[7] – Hilda spent much of the journey writing poetry. She was 24 years old when they landed at Le Havre. She confessed to Frances that she had no intention of ever returning to live in the United States.[8]

France was everything they had hoped for. The two snuck off to take nude photographs of one another on the beach, went to museums, and heatedly debated art and aesthetics, touring France with guidebooks firmly in hand. They nearly missed the Louvre, for it had closed in late July after the *Mona Lisa* was stolen, but they eagerly returned when it reopened. There they viewed the *Sleeping Hermaphroditus*, an ancient marble statue that made quite an impression on them, for it appears in subsequent works by both. In Frances's poem, the *Hermaphroditus* is an ideal figure – 'all parts of thee attuned', it contains 'all this pulsing world'.[9] The two venerated the androgyne at this point in their lives. 'I see you. I feel you,' Hermione tells Fayne (Frances) in H.D.'s autobiographical novel *Asphodel*, 'I don't want to be (as they say crudely) a boy. Nor do I want you so to be. I don't feel a girl.'[10]

Le Havre, Étaples, Rouen, Paris, Versailles. At Rouen, they honoured the site of the execution of the cross-dressing Joan of Arc, a figure who captivated H.D. throughout her life.[11] Hilda identified with Joan of Arc because of her heterodox views on gender and religion. 'They had trapped her, a girl who was a boy and they would always do that,' H.D. writes in *Asphodel*: 'They would always trap them, bash their heads like broken flowers from their stalks, break them for seeing things, having "visions" seeing things . . . I don't want to be burnt, to be crucified just because I "see" things sometimes.' For H.D., the institution of Christianity was to blame, not Christ: 'I don't think Fayne Rabb realized . . . how I love her,' she wrote of Frances, but 'Christ would understand.'[12]

At Rouen, Frances experienced a life-changing revelation about religion, art and her purpose in life that placed her decidedly at odds with Hilda. From that point forward, their paths forked – artistically to be sure, but also in terms of how they would conduct their romantic lives. In Frances's view, Hilda had resolved that

art should come before everything. The artists were the vanguard of consciousness. Goodness and evil did not matter. Sex did matter, for its colour and richness fed the senses as nothing else did. Sex should be treated, and developed, as an Art. Responsibilities, relatives, fidelities, none of these things mattered.

But Frances had come to see that, for her, a quest for beauty was not enough; she wanted to spend her life addressing social ills in 'a world of wars and sickness, cruelty, starvation, and inequality of means'. She also wanted a family and children.[13] This divergence in views, so excruciatingly exposed in this singular moment, would come to mean the demise of their relationship. Though the two would continue to struggle with an unhealthy mutual obsession with one another for many years to come, this moment foretold an ending. It bespoke a fundamentally incompatible vision of their future selves.

Both Frances and H.D. record the latter's commitment to writing. If Gregg found herself 'inarticulate' in the quiet churches of the French countryside, Hilda was always scribbling poems in her diary. 'That was Hilda', Gregg remembered: 'lissome, curved, withdrawn, writing assiduously'.[14] From Rouen, the trio travelled to Paris, staying initially, unknowingly, in a house of prostitution in Montmartre, before bedbugs (if *Asphodel* is to be believed) drove them to better lodgings. The Greggs were not wealthy: Julia was a schoolteacher and a single mother. None of the three was savvy about international travel. H.D. later romanticized their shoddy lodgings: 'I love the sordid touch . . . It gives character, poignancy and point to all this. And we live on nothing.'[15] But she was nonetheless grateful when they encountered by chance Walter Rummel, a Paris-based composer and musician they had met in Philadelphia with Pound, who taught them to better navigate the city. Rummel had a studio in a Parisian suburb near the Seine, where he played piano for the threesome. While he and Hilda conversed about art and music, Frances and Julia had tea, or sat under the glaring microscope of Rummel's and H.D.'s collective gaze: 'there was perfect comprehension and union between them, and I was not of them,' Frances recalled bitterly.[16] A year later, on a return trip to Paris, Rummel and Hilda collaborated on five songs for children that exhibit themes – otherworldliness and the violence of nature among them – that would imbue H.D.'s first volume of poetry, *Sea Garden*.[17]

Arriving in London in early October, Hilda and Frances were thrust into a whirlwind of social invitations arranged by Ezra

Pound, an experience at once exhilarating and intimidating. Hilda remembered a rather awkward entrance into the salons of the European avant-garde, a series of humiliations over her national identity and her cumbersome moniker. In *Paint It Today*, H.D.'s alter-ego, Midget, offers a sense of how mortifying she found these trials:

> People called me Miss Defreddie, which was surely not a
> name, or if it was a name it was a thing to be laughed at.
> If people laughed I was embarrassed and tried to laugh
> with them as if I had never heard just that laugh at just
> that particular name before. If they did not laugh, it was
> equally embarrassing, because one wondered if they had
> not heard properly, or if they were concealing the laugh
> and would suddenly burst forth with it like someone who
> has inadvertently swallowed a bit of hot potato.[18]

But Frances remembered her presence quite differently; that Hilda so easily integrated into the artistic circles of Paris and London, she recalls, was quite difficult for herself and her mother. 'Hilda was far more adroit than I at picking up the patter of this group,' Gregg observed with regards to a party at the home of novelist May Sinclair: 'It was almost a code that they had evolved from the technicalities of their trade . . . Grammar, syntax, punctuation were the dragons to be slain by these knights of the pen.'[19]

Indeed, Hilda's initiation into these rarefied circles was the subject of a number of scarcely fictionalized portraits in this period, the most scathing, perhaps, in a 1916 novel by Frances's future husband, dedicated to Frances and undoubtedly co-written with her. In *The Buffoon*, Hilda appears as Eunice Dinwiddie, a young American poet who exerts control over her image with 'studied artlessness', playing the part of the beautiful, brilliant and mysterious ingénue. Pound is duly eviscerated as the 'spiritually cocky' Raoul Root, an uncouth showman touting his artistic wares with outlandish affectations and an improbably vertical hairstyle. Eunice's flowing costumes, her 'delicately calculated' entrances, her staged swoonings and lyrical flights of fancy, even her hushed, trembling voice, make her the undeniable centre of attention in every room, but these features conceal 'hard, cold' eyes and boundless ambition.[20] The portrait is greatly exaggerated, but it does suggest that Hilda, naturally shy, had developed an effective strategy for confronting these daunting situations that she found so appalling. It prefigures her later success as an actor, but it also suggests the extent to which Ezra used her, as an advertisement for his own projects, and she him, to establish herself in London's literary circles and further her career.

This mocking depiction was to come later on, however, in a relationship that would continue to be tumultuous. In the autumn of 1911 in England, despite their disagreements over art and life, Frances and Hilda suffered an agonizing parting as the Greggs returned to the United States. In vain, Hilda had pleaded with them not to leave, but Julia needed to return to her job. As the fateful day approached, Hilda tried to convince Frances to remain behind, staging a dramatic scene that she was well aware Frances would appreciate. 'I, Hermione, tell you I love you Fayne,' reads a frantic stream-of-consciousness passage in *Asphodel*. Though men may claim to love her, they cannot match Hermione's passion: 'Will anyone ever say I love you Fayne as I say it?' The two did consider living together in London. Fayne suggests ways to screen their relationship from the world in such a scenario, but Hilda's character responds vehemently, and naively, that there was no need for such contrivances: 'What have we done or could we do to need any apology or explanation? I am burning away that's all . . . I don't want you to miss it. I'm going to write, work.'[21] In the end, Frances departed Liverpool for the States on the *Mauretania*, promising to return the following spring. When she did make that voyage again, she would arrive in London as Mrs Louis Wilkinson.

After Frances's departure, Hilda continued to write, spending her days in the British Museum. Spurred in part by Ezra's preference for Frances's poetry the previous year, she was determined to hone her craft, confident of eventual success. She also continued to circulate among the London literati. Pound had introduced her to Brigit Patmore, who promptly took Hilda under her wing. Born Ethel Elizabeth Morrison-Scott in 1882 in Ireland and married to Coventry Patmore's grandson, Brigit was a fledgling writer, feminist and perpetual hostess of parties and salons that brought together English artists and writers, as well as suffragettes and others interested in women's issues.[22] Hilda's arrival in London was just weeks before more than two hundred suffragettes were arrested for a window-breaking campaign, and this was surely a topic of conversation at gatherings at the Patmore home in north Kensington that autumn.

Hilda was no political radical – Brigit, May Sinclair, Violet Hunt, these writers were publicly outspoken about women's rights – but she would spend her life writing about sex and gender, and the suffragist cause interested her. She attended a suffragette meeting with the novelist John Galsworthy's sister, Lilian Sauter, another hostess, in November of 1911,[23] and she registered to vote in London in the year women's suffrage became law under the Representation of the People Act of 1918. Her early short story 'The Suffragette' savagely satirizes upper-crust women opposing suffrage and features the coming-to-feminist-consciousness of a young, naive American girl in London who decides to attend a suffragette meeting after a friend explains that 'men are able at a moment's notice to get work' but impoverished women 'who do the same work, and sometimes do it better', are unable to secure employment.[24]

Brigit was, by all accounts, charismatic and stunningly beautiful, and she was enraptured with Hilda. Her 1926 book *This Impassioned Onlooker* encodes a dedication to Hilda's 'loveliness greater than the heartrending beauty of the world', a sanitized version of verbiage so blatantly homoerotic that she had been forced to change it.[25] It was Brigit who introduced Hilda to her future husband, the dashing nineteen-year-old writer Richard Aldington, with whom Brigit had already had an affair. Richard thought Brigit was in love with Hilda, while Hilda, wary of Brigit's purported bisexuality, suspected she was in love with Richard. Indeed, in H.D.'s autobiographical fiction about the period, the character based on Brigit hops back and forth between Richard's and Hilda's beds. Brigit would nonetheless continue to be a close friend to Hilda until the late 1920s, when Brigit and Richard began a decade-long affair that would sever irrevocably her intimate friendship with Hilda.

In the spring of 1912, when she met Richard, Hilda was ready for a new relationship, for she had been shaken by the announcement of Frances's sudden marriage and her return to London.[26] When Frances and her new husband invited her along on their honeymoon to Belgium and Italy, Ezra convinced her not to go. She was surprised to learn from Ezra that Frances and Wilkinson's closest friend, the writer John Cowper Powys, were embroiled in a passionate affair. After the honeymooners departed London to meet Powys in Italy, Hilda left, alone, for an extended trip to Paris, taking refuge at the same rue Jacob flat where she and Frances had lived the previous year. Alone, mired in 'great turmoil – confusion – weariness' over Frances's marriage, she was delighted when Aldington joined her in mid-May.[27] They strolled along the Seine and visited the city's famous museums. 'To look at beautiful things with H.D. is a remarkable experience,' Aldington reflected years later: 'She responds so swiftly, understands so perfectly, re-lives the artist's mood so intensely, that the work of art seems transformed.'[28] Despite – or perhaps in part because of – the suicide of her friend Margaret Cravens, a pianist, in early June in Paris, Hilda and Aldington grew closer.

Born Edward Godfree Aldington in 1892, Richard had grown up in Portsmouth, Deal and Dover, the son of a solicitor and a sensational novelist, and the eldest of four children. His parents were a constant source of frustration for him, his father because of his disastrous financial dealings, and his working-class mother because of what Aldington's biographer refers to as her 'dubious moral conduct'.[29] Later, looking back over three decades, Richard imagines with amusement his destiny had he not rebelled against them: he would have been 'a fairly prosperous provincial lawyer', a conservative churchgoer, a golfer and a drinker.[30] From a young age, however, he was determined to resist that fate and become a writer. Both of his parents had literary aspirations, but Richard had to become a working writer at an early age, his father having gone into debt suddenly and unexpectedly while Richard was still at University College in London. Richard resented leaving university, where he had been studying the classics. He and Hilda shared an ardour for the ancient Greeks, Euripides in particular. At eighteen, Richard had penned his first free verse, inspired by the playwright's *Hippolytus*.[31] He joined Hilda daily at the British Museum. In the Reading Room, she copied materials for him; six years her junior, he was not yet old enough to possess a reader card of his own.[32]

John Gould Fletcher remembers the two as opposites:

> They were, it seemed to me, an oddly assorted couple, providing a complete contrast. While H.D. was tall, slim, lithe, with a pale oval face framed in masses of dark hair, and a nervous shyness of manner that only emphasized her fragility, Aldington was bluff, hearty, and robust, with the square shoulders of an athlete, the bullethead of a guardsman, and a general tendency to beefiness which proclaimed his British quality.[33]

Or, as another friend, James Whitall, put it: 'it would have been hard to find two other such irresistible people as temperamentally dissimilar.'[34] In the early years of their courtship, they seemed very well suited for one another, their differences complementary rather than inharmonious. 'I had never met anyone in my life before who understood the other half or the explanatory quarter of the part of the sentences I left unsaid,' H.D. wrote of a character based on Richard in one of her autobiographical novels.[35]

If the couple lacked the emotional intensity she and Frances had shared, they were exceptionally compatible intellectually and in their shared dedication to discovering and expressing beauty, adhering to a philosophy of life Frances had categorically rejected. In *Asphodel*, H.D. described a figure as committed to art as she was: 'His love had been that rapture of some wild young thing and she had liked him, loved him because he was wild and didn't do the right thing and hated his family . . . for they had tried to spoil his writing, hadn't wanted him to write.'[36] Writing was everything, they agreed, and they shared an unshakable work ethic. In his 1941 memoir *Life for Life's Sake*, Aldington recalls,

> H.D. showed an original sensitive mind and an almost faultless craftsmanship. This craftsmanship was the result of infinite pains. Version after version of a poem was discarded by H.D. in the search for perfection, and the pruning was ruthless . . . I was staggered by this relentless artistic conscience.[37]

He was the perfect companion for Ezra as well, who affectionately dubbed Richard 'Faun', though the term took on a much more condescending cast when their relationship soured in the years to follow. In 1912 and 1913, however, Ezra, Hilda and Richard were inseparable, working and living in adjacent flats of the same building in Kensington. Before Hilda had arrived in Europe, Pound had been trying to envision a 'new poetry', spending evenings with W. B. Yeats and the philosopher-poet T. E. Hulme, discussing possibilities. But this 'new poetry' did not really take shape until he and Hilda were reunited and he began spending time with her and Richard. Looking back, in 1929, Aldington claimed that Pound's theories were based on H.D.'s practice.[38] Cyrena Pondrom concurs: 'Pound's own understandings of what modern poetry should be trying to do significantly depended upon the models which H.D.'s poems offered him.'[39]

Together, then, in 1912, the threesome devised the principles of Imagism, the movement that would introduce the world to English-language *vers libre*. 'They dealt a blow at the post-Victorian magazine poets . . . They made free verse popular,' Aldington was to sum up its impact.[40] Famously, at the British Museum tearoom – Americans H.D. and Pound 'took an insane relish for afternoon tea'[41] – the decision was made to send three of H.D.'s poems (and, later, three of Aldington's) to *Poetry* editor Harriet Monroe to inaugurate a movement dedicated to the primacy of the object, to sparseness of language and to rhythm based not on a regular pattern but a musical score. Pound withdrew his own poems from submission, sent to Monroe earlier, when he realized that H.D.'s were the more apt exemplars – the material embodiment of their collective theoretical imaginings. H.D.'s poems appeared in *Poetry* in January 1913, and Imagism was launched.

Poetry magazine had begun just a few months earlier with the promise that poetry was for the public, offering an 'open door' to new poets: 'May the great poet we are looking for never find it shut, or half-shut, against his ample genius!'[42] The three poems by H.D. – 'Hermes of the Ways', 'Priapus' and 'Epigram' – were the only poems in the issue without a regular metre and rhyme scheme. It is difficult for us to imagine, more than a century later, just how perverse free verse seemed at that time. Free verse was linked to free love, suffragism, anarchism, political radicalism and any number of other movements that shocked both popular audiences and established writers of the period. It was nothing short of a revolution.

H.D.'s poetry arguably initiated modernist free verse in English. Pound had published a few free-verse poems prior to January

1913, but, as Pondrom points out, verse by Pound and Aldington at this time was still laden with sentiment – still bore a taint of Victorian sensibility – while H.D.'s poems were clear, direct and 'crystalline', the last a descriptor so oft-used that she would later come to resent it as a label she could not shake. The best-known of the three poems, 'Hermes of the Ways', opens at the shoreline, with the 'break[ing]' of 'hard sand' into something beautiful and intoxicating, 'clear as wine'. The ancient Greek god who bridges the heavens and the earth, Hermes, stands at the borderland between sea and land, sheltered. This focus on liminality – where water meets sand, sky meets earth, 'Where sea-grass tangles with/ Shore-grass' – permeates all of H.D.'s early verse. The poem offers a battered landscape, apples struggling to ripen against the forces of sea and sun, trees 'twisted' by the wind.[43]

As H.D.'s poems were making their way across the Atlantic to *Poetry*, her parents were planning a lengthy trip abroad. They had only reluctantly conceded to permit their unmarried daughter to remain in Europe when the Greggs departed, and they were determined to act as chaperone and then convince her to return home. (In that era, H.D.'s decision to stay in Europe after the Greggs' departure was unconventional at best, scandalous at worst.) In October of 1912, H.D. met them in Genoa and the reunited family travelled to Florence, Rome, Naples and Venice, with Ezra and Richard joining them at various points along the way. In July, Helen and Charles Doolittle continued on to the Alps, and H.D. and Richard returned to London, via Paris, to get back to work. In addition to writing more poems in the Imagist vein, she was intent on translating her favourite ancient Greek dramatist, Euripides, whose work she would read, reread and translate throughout her life. Decades later, Richard remembered the spring of 1913 as 'the happiest of his life'.[44]

When her parents finally made their way to England in September of 1913, Hilda and Richard pre-empted her parents' plea for her return to the States by announcing their intent to marry in just one month's time. But this was a plan that had been hatched in the spring of 1912 in Paris, before their arrival, for Hilda had no intention of returning to the smothering atmosphere of her parents' household.[45] There were to be no festivities – on that point Hilda was insistent: 'I won't be engaged. But I'm going to marry [him] . . . Just marry him,' her alter-ego declares in *Paint It Today*.[46] So, with Ezra and her parents as their only witnesses, the two were married in the Kensington registry office on 18 October 1913. (Richard's parents may or may not have been notified, but they were not present.[47]) The marriage was an act that would ultimately prove liberatory, shielding her sexual relationships with women and men in the decades to come. Newly wedded, H.D. and Richard moved a short distance away from their flat at Kensington Church Walk to Holland Place Chambers. Surprising the Aldingtons, Ezra trailed behind them upon his own marriage to Dorothy Shakespear six months later, moving to their building, where he would begin the *Cantos*. It was also during this time that H.D. and Richard worked as amanuenses for their friend Ford Madox Hueffer (Ford) as he drafted his best-known novel, *The Good Soldier*.

Frances and Louis Wilkinson promptly installed themselves in H.D.'s old flat at Kensington Walk, following a rowdy honeymoon trip during which Frances had been arrested by Venetian police for cross-dressing.[48] Frances had not disappeared from Hilda's life, and she also wanted to be a writer. Her verse, too, appeared in the prominent 'little magazines' *Poetry* and *Others*. A poem scribbled in the margins of her copy of *Sea Garden*, 'My Hilda', attests to the idealism and passion of their shared youth: 'the life in me leaps/ to the sound of our dreams.' 'My aching dry lips reach out/ For you in the dusk,' she pleads, 'Touch them with wine.'[49] 'To H.D.', however, printed in *Poetry*, is at once a public tribute and a finely honed dagger. It begins with an apostrophe to Hilda:

You were all loveliness to me –
Sea-mist, the spring,
The blossoming of trees,
The wind,
Giver-of-Dreams.

But a turn in the poem assigns blame for the end of their romance
on Hilda's 'wistful silence':

Your beauty burned and wrought me
Into a bell,
Whose single note
Was echo of your silence.

She closes by recasting and ironizing H.D.'s line from 'Orchard':
'Spare us from loveliness!'[50] Frances never forgot – and never failed to
remind Hilda of – their aesthetic differences and the tragedy of their
past. H.D., though ever loyal to Frances, was at times tortured by her
cruelty. In Gregg's poem, H.D. 'sign[s]' while Frances is 'muted'. It
was H.D., not Frances, who was finding success as an Imagist.

Every avant-garde movement needs a manifesto and a platform.
If *Poetry* was the vehicle for Imagism's beginnings, it was a rebranded
permutation of Dora Marsden's *Freewoman* – to become the *New
Freewoman* and, later, *The Egoist* – that became Imagism's principal
organ. Born in 1882, Marsden was raised in a working-class family
in Yorkshire and became an educator, suffragette and philosopher.
Having been expelled from the Women's Social and Political Union,
a militant organization devoted to women's suffrage, Marsden
founded *The Freewoman* to give voice to a form of feminism that
was more diverse and class-conscious than that of the Union. The
periodical ran for a year, but she was ultimately unable to keep it
going after its distributor WHSmith banned it due to its progressive
economic and cultural views. In the meantime, Marsden and

a very young Rebecca West had been discussing art as a site of revolutionary potential. West had the opportunity to introduce Marsden to Pound at a party thrown by Violet Hunt, a fellow suffragette and writer, and Ford Madox Hueffer's extramarital companion.[51] Pound brought not only a keen eye for literary talent but some financial support to the foundering periodical. The *New Freewoman* commenced publication in June 1913.

West introduced Imagism to the readership of the *New Freewoman* two months later, in the 15 August issue of the magazine. 'Poetry should be burned to the bone by austere fires and washed white with rains of affliction,' West avers in her article's opening, 'But there has arisen a little band who desire the poet to be as disciplined and efficient as a stevedore.' Quoting liberally from manifestos by Pound and by the poet and translator F. S. Flint that had previously appeared in *Poetry*, West described the 'new poetry' and offered a few 'don'ts' from Pound, who advised budding poets to avoid abstractions and ornamentation, and to cultivate a strong work ethic.[52] When, the following year, the publication changed names, Pound suggested Harriet Weaver as its editor and Aldington as one of its assistant editors, freeing up Marsden to focus on her writing. A few poems by Pound, Aldington and H.D. had appeared on the pages of the *New Freewoman*, but, in its first year, Imagist poetry appeared in nearly every issue of *The Egoist*. It also printed James Joyce's *Portrait of the Artist as a Young Man* in serial form.

Before the First World War, H.D. was publishing poems in the little magazines *Poetry, New Freewoman, The Egoist* and the short-lived *Glebe*, an American avant-garde periodical edited by writer Alfred Kreymborg and artist Man Ray, who were ecstatic about Imagism. She was gaining a modest following among other young writers, but the publication of her first book of poetry, *Sea Garden*, would introduce her work to a much wider audience. Though it was published in 1916, much of the verse had been composed in the years before the war.[53]

The poems of *Sea Garden* swirl around images constantly in motion, hardly the static ones Pound had initially created in his own work. The volume is beautifully crafted, carefully assembled. It represents, as Lesley Wheeler has argued, 'the poetry volume as an ecosystem, in which the poem-organisms coexist in delicate interdependence . . . an environment, resonant with echoes, that demands exploration.'[54] It dwells in that netherworld between sea and land, that liminal space in which 'the hard sand breaks' under the force of waves. The flora of this landscape is not so much wind-swept as wind-ravaged, battered, 'marred', 'caught in the drift', 'stunted', 'flung on the sand', 'slashed and torn'.[55] But though their 'grasp is frail', these sea flowers (mostly) survive, 'torn, twisted/ but showing the fight was valiant'.[56] It is this battered, wild vegetation her speakers revere – 'a new beauty/ in some terrible/ wind-tortured place' – not the cultivated flowers of the domesticated garden.[57] That is 'beauty without strength'; her speakers want 'wind to break', to 'scatter these pink-stalks,/ snap off their spiced heads'.[58] As Fletcher observes in his review of the book, her flowers are 'made perfect and unfading through their own exceeding bitterness'.[59] H.D. is revising centuries of romantic poetry about flowers, countering rose with sea rose, finding beauty in debris left in the wake of a storm.

H.D.'s ancient Greece is a world suffused with spiritual presence. The speakers in *Sea Garden* do not shy away from the violence of nature, orchestrated by gods and demigods who flit across the land, emerge from briny water and hover at the tops of trees. The space between sea and land is a space of danger. Rocks may shelter ships, or they may 'cut and wreck' them.[60] Storms 'crash over the trees' and 'crack the live branch', rendering 'each leaf . . . rent like split wood'.[61] Like the blossoms of this sea garden, snapped from their stems, sailors and woodsmen are intrepid but ultimately helpless. The sea takes its victims, the gods 'hav[ing] invented/ curious torture for us', and those who survive – 'flayed' both by nature and by the intensity of its beauty – strive to propitiate the gods, making desperate and reverent offerings.[62] As the poet Amy Lowell pointed out in her own analysis of H.D.'s work, 'To this poet, beauty is a thing so sharp as to be painful, delight so poignant it can scarcely be borne. Her extreme sensitiveness turns appreciation to exquisite suffering. Yet, again and again, she flings herself bravely upon the spears of her own reactions.'[63] As the volume gradually moves inland, the reader is readied for the shift from coast to 'Cities', the title of the volume's final poem. The busy, congested man-made environs are an ambiguous haven, 'so full/ that men could not grasp beauty'. It is left to poets to both 'recall the old splendour' and 'await the new beauty of cities'.[64]

Sea Garden came out with Constable Press in the UK, which had long been dedicated to publishing fine literature for the mass market, and Houghton Mifflin in the United States. H.D.'s audience had suddenly expanded beyond the cultivated readership of little magazines. The *Times Literary Supplement* was generally critical of *Sea Garden*. The reviewer found Imagism inscrutable, taking issue with the elusiveness and 'confused obscurity' of modern poetry. There is much fretting about pronoun referents. The poet, the reviewer complains, 'often leaves us puzzled as to what he wants to express by his images'.[65] This response was typical of reviewers in mainstream publications of that era, who simply did not yet know what to make of free verse. 'Imagism is presentation, not representation,' Lowell would attempt to explain in 1917, but it would take some time before the 'new poetry' would find acceptance outside of small avant-garde circles.[66]

H.D. was undaunted. She was ahead of her time. The reviewer's assumption that H.D. was a man was a supposition she did little to discount. She was, after all, an androgyne. Her work – despite, or perhaps because of, this presumption of male authorship – was being taken seriously at last. She had broken with Pound and was standing on her own.

3

'the black cloud fell', 1914–18

On 28 June 1914, the heir to the throne of Austria–Hungary was
assassinated by a Bosnian Serb, a member of a Yugoslav nationalist
political group, in an act of defiance against Austro-Hungarian
rule in the Balkans. A domino effect ensued as a complex network
of alliances between European countries drew the continent
reluctantly into declarations of war. On 4 August, in response to
German aggression towards politically neutral Belgium, Britain
formally entered the fray. That evening, H.D. and Richard could
be found in the 'mob scene', amidst the jubilant crowd of people
outside Buckingham Palace who sang the National Anthem and
cheered as the royal family ceremoniously appeared on their
balcony.[1] Richard's autobiographical account of the period dates
his apprehension about what was to come to that moment in July,
when 'Newspapers suddenly became important.' From the very
beginning of the war, he had 'a fatalistic instinct that sooner or
later I should be involved in the massacre'.[2] As fellow Imagist John
Gould Fletcher recalls, after the outbreak of war, Richard was 'no
longer the gay, insouciant, jaunty, swaggering Aldington I had
known'.[3] But it would be two more years before Richard enlisted.
In the meantime, he and H.D. continued writing and promoting
Imagism. For the Aldingtons, however, the most momentous event
of 1914 was H.D.'s pregnancy.

Within Imagism, tensions with Ezra Pound were rising to
intolerable levels, and with a baby coming, the Aldingtons moved

'away from Kensingtonian squabbles and intrigues' to a larger flat in Hampstead, near the Heath.[4] But 'squabbles' proved impossible to avoid. Undaunted by their move, Ezra was still rushing in and out of their home with alarming frequency, seeking feedback on his Chinese translations and exclaiming his grandiose plans for the future of modern poetry.[5] While H.D. and Richard exercised patience with Pound, F. S. Flint, Aldington's closest comrade among their fellow Imagists, waged the most volatile disagreements with him. After one particularly virulent exchange between Pound and Flint over the origins of the movement, H.D. attempted to soothe Flint, encouraging diplomacy: 'We are both so angry – though we wouldn't have E.P. know we are annoyed for the world – silence is the best, for us, I think, and surely the simplest policy!'[6] H.D. was by nature non-confrontational and rarely burned bridges, but privately she was growing tired of Ezra's antics: 'We can't go on watching him like two keepers – can we?'[7]

The Imagists argued about the past, present and future of the movement. One heated point of dispute concerned the selection of poems to include in anthologies. The volume *Des Imagistes*, which appeared with Charles and Albert Boni in 1914, had been compiled entirely by Pound, who selected poems by himself, Aldington, H.D., Flint, Ford Madox Ford, James Joyce, Amy Lowell, Allen Upward and William Carlos Williams. The American public responded eagerly and variously – with enthusiasm, consternation and antagonism – while the British largely ignored it. Aldington's review of the volume praised H.D.'s poetry above the rest, comparing her verse to 'nicely-carved marble' and declaring it 'as good a specimen of Imagism as can be found'.[8]

However, as with most of this era's avant-garde movements, Imagism began to come apart at the very instant it established itself. From the moment Boston poet Amy Lowell met Pound, the end of Imagism was preordained. An unapologetic lesbian, Lowell had a personality so eccentric that it rivalled Pound's. She was

H.D., late 1910s.

large and brash, she smoked cigars and she appeared in public with her lifelong partner, Ada Russell. She was also wealthy, and Pound initially saw her as a source of funds for the movement and the various modernist periodicals with which he was affiliated, but in short time Lowell and Pound began to tussle over the reins. (Rebecca West had long since resigned her editorial post due to Pound's heavy-handed involvement.)

If she did not always live up to her own principles, Amy Lowell argued for what she described as a more democratic process, in which poets would select their own contributions. Everyone (save Harriet Monroe) sided with her. The newly organized Imagists, under Lowell's leadership and H.D. and Richard's editorial eyes, published *Some Imagist Poets* in April 1915, with Ferris Greenslet at Houghton Mifflin, to even more success and controversy than Pound's inaugural volume had garnered. It included poems by H.D., Aldington, Fletcher, Flint, Lowell and D. H. Lawrence, but none by Pound; 481 of its 750 copies pre-sold.[9] In Pound's mind, Lowell had 'hijack[ed]' his movement,[10] but in fact he had become so controlling and cantankerous that he had alienated them all. 'Ezra', Aldington put it succinctly, 'was a bit of a czar.'[11]

As their work became more widely read, another battle raged in the pages of the *New Republic*. The American writer Conrad Aiken (who would later befriend H.D.) vilified the Imagists as a 'very loud-voiced little mutual-admiration society', as makers of 'frail pictures' with 'a gentle preciosity of sound and colour' who capture only 'the semi-precious in experience'.[12] But his scathing review only served to generate more publicity, and Lowell's friend William Braithwaite, a Black poet, editor and literary critic, defended the movement one month later. He was a surprising ally, as he himself admired more conventional verse forms. But he took a strong position, addressing each of Aiken's criticisms and comparing the young poets to the finest in English literary history:

All really great poets have broken the traditional regularities of forms handed on to them by their predecessors; they found their genius could not achieve within the restrictions, and instead of adding to the mediocrity of the art, imposed technical obligations upon themselves which only the most rigorous and persistent labors could accomplish. This, it seems to me, is what the imagists are doing. It is what Chaucer, Shakespeare, Coleridge, Blake, Poe and Henley have done.

'I approached the work of the imagists with considerable doubt,' Braithwaite admitted, 'but soon found myself surrendering to an influence that was different from any other in the poetry of the day . . . it was a force, an element, which created beauty on a strange new pattern.'[13]

Meanwhile, Pound and Wyndham Lewis – that prickly young artist who occasionally wandered into the Aldington flat to borrow Richard's razor[14] – were planning the first issue of *BLAST*, which launched Vorticism, a movement not wholly unlike Imagism but with a focus on dynamism, energy and movement, and a strong British nationalist and masculinist bent. Its manifesto decried 'effeminate' culture and scorned all art of continental Europe, proclaiming, 'The Modern World is due almost entirely to Anglo-Saxon genius.'[15] Aldington signed the Vorticist manifesto. H.D. did not, though it did not stop Pound from using her poem 'Oread' as exemplar of the new movement.[16] The war between Pound and Lowell reached farcical heights in the summer of 1914 when celebratory dinners for Vorticism and Imagism were held two days apart at the London theatre restaurant Dieudonné, long known for its patronage by artists and performers and its openness to women dining alone. Accounts vary widely, but it seems certain that Pound satirized his old group by donning a tin bathtub on his head and announcing the mock birth of 'nageism', taking the French word for swimming to craft a spiteful reference to the uproar over Lowell's

'In the Garden', in which the speaker yearns to see her lover bathing in a pool: readers had been shocked at the image of a nude woman of Lowell's ample girth.[17] Pound's mean-spirited antics did little to mend the rift.

The beginning of the First World War, and the internal and external discord around Imagism, meant that 1914 and 1915 were stressful years for the Aldingtons. In May 1915, H.D. suffered a stillbirth, two weeks after the sinking of the *Lusitania*. One of the largest passenger ships in the world, RMS *Lusitania* was torpedoed by a German U-boat, resulting in the deaths of more than 1,000 people. This blatant attack deliberately targeting an unarmed ship full of civilians generated a public outcry against the Germans, who countered that the ship was carrying munitions; in fact, it was, though the British government denied it at the time. The act transpired on the heels of the German army's use of chlorine gas on Allied troops, the first instance of modern chemical warfare. H.D. blamed the shock of the *Lusitania* incident for the stillbirth.

Richard was bereaved by their loss: 'I have been rather distressed, because Hilda was delivered of a little girl still-born, about 2 a.m. this morning . . . I haven't seen the doctor, but the nurse said it was a beautiful child & they can't think why it didn't live. It was very strong, but couldn't breathe.'[18] Years later, H.D. would fictionalize this experience. In *Asphodel*, her narrator reports being shamed by nurses for having a vocation. In frustration, Hermione cries, 'Was there nothing else in the world? Men and guns, women and babies. And if you have a mind what then?'[19] In the hospital scenes of the autobiographically based *Bid Me to Live* and *Asphodel*, H.D.'s narrator is told that her life will be in grave danger if she becomes pregnant again during the war, prompting a reluctant cessation of her sexual relationship with her husband. The marriage bed becomes the 'death-bed': 'Sheets, a bed, a tomb'.[20] Her depiction of the aftermath of the stillbirth has led to speculation that H.D. and Aldington's physical relationship did in fact suffer for this reason and led, indirectly, to two extramarital affairs on his part. It is also likely that their old friend, the hostess and writer Brigit Patmore, 'comforted' Richard sexually while H.D. recovered, incurring the wrath of T. S. Eliot.[21]

H.D. remained in hospital until 11 June, when she was well enough to leave and go to the countryside with Aldington. There, for a few months, she was to recover physically and emotionally, and she was able to do so away from the Zeppelin raids that had begun in London in May. The worst of those raids occurred in early September, and Aldington reported a frightening day when their offices at *The Egoist* saw damage:

> My God, we had shrapnel bursting over head for 15 minutes, and saw the Zeppelin wondering where it would plant its next bomb! The Post Office was just missed; Wood St., Cheapside is burnt to the ground; an immense warehouse in Farringdon Road is smashed & every window for a hundred yards around broken; Queen's Square has a bomb in the middle of it, every window in the Square smashed, frames & doors broken – one window of the Poetry Bookshop smashed![22]

Summer in the country was ideal for the period of grieving that the two needed. Letters to friends in June and July emphasize the healing power of nature in their new environs in Kent and then Surrey, which were lush with late spring flora. Just as importantly, they were also able to return to work, which for H.D. would nearly always prove restorative. It was in Surrey that they began to imagine a Poets' Translation Series for themselves, Flint and their friends James Whitall and Edward Storer. (Though the series would ultimately bear Aldington's name, Caroline Zilboorg characterizes H.D. as an unacknowledged co-editor.)[23] The goal of the series was to translate lesser-known ancient Greek and Latin writers into English – they both loved Meleager's *Greek Anthology* for its compilation of

the work of so many men and women writers of the ancient era
– in order to demonstrate that the literary efforts of the ancient
Greeks were 'more alive, more essential, more human' than English
literature.[24] They viewed their translation work as 'bringing the
past into the present, the Hellenic into modernist poetry'.[25] But
H.D. made the surprising choice to translate Euripides – whom
she deemed 'a freethinker, and an iconoclast'[26] – for the project, an
ambitious move that put her in competition with renowned classicist
Gilbert Murray, whose own translation of Euripides was then well
known and respected.

To a greater extent than any of her previous work, *Choruses
from Iphigeneia in Aulis*, H.D.'s liberal translation of Euripides into
modern English free-verse poetry, responded to the First World
War. *Iphigeneia in Aulis* was the first Euripides play she had ever
seen performed, at the age of sixteen, a performance in which Ezra
cross-dressed.[27] For the series, H.D. selected choruses from the
play, exploring the collective voice of a community of women on
the brink of war. 'H.D.'s interest in the Euripidean chorus is tied
to her deliberate lyric experimentation,' Eileen Gregory observes,
'an effort to find polyphony in lyric voice and complexity in lyric
temporality and spatiality'.[28] She was reimagining the scope of the
lyric 'I' in a time that called for a communal response.

The play recounts Agamemnon's decision to sacrifice his
daughter, Iphigeneia, to mollify an enraged Artemis, who had
obstructed Greek passage to Troy. H.D.'s first chorus of the
women of Chalkis is set on the border between sea and land,
where luminous warships and robust, striking warriors assemble
in an erotically charged scene that lures the Greek women into a
violent complicity. As in *Sea Garden*, the women are flayed by a
double-edged beauty: 'This beauty is too much/ For any woman./
It is burnt across my eyes.'[29] The second brief chorus shifts to 'the
bulwarks of Troy', the scene of Paris's seduction of Helen, exposing
the mutual desire that caused the Greeks to 'snatch up their

spears'.[30] The third chorus imagines the inevitable Greek invasion of Troy and the return of Helen to Greek shores, the 'bright stain' left on 'stone-battlements', the pain of the Trojan queen and her daughters, Helen's lament and the enslavement of the Trojans.[31] But it also calls into question men's truth, demanding to know 'where truth is' and asking, 'Of what use is valour?'[32] H.D.'s translation closes with Iphigeneia of the 'stained throat' as the true hero of the battle. 'I come', she intones, as she embraces her fate, 'I destroy Phrygia and all Troy.'[33]

During the war years, H.D. published poems in *Poetry*, *The Egoist*, the *Little Review*, *Greenwich Village* and Harriet Monroe and Alice Corbin Henderson's *The New Poetry*, winning awards at both *Poetry* and the *Little Review*. But it was her translation of Euripides that had the greatest impact on her burgeoning reputation. In an unsigned review in the *Times Literary Supplement* by the esteemed biographer and education reformer J. W. Mackail, H.D. received more praise than she had for her free-verse poetry volume of the same year. While Mackail's review is not entirely appreciative – he expresses some disdain for the lack of competence in ancient languages exhibited by all of the group – his review singles out H.D.'s volume from the rest of the series as demonstrating 'surprising novelty and interest' and 'an interpretive genius which is both provocative and singularly illuminating'. Her work proves, he avers, 'the power of classical poetry to give each generation a new thrill, to kindle the spirit of poetry over and over again from their own elemental and perdurable fire'.[34] T. S. Eliot's review of *Choruses* in *Poetry* went further, comparing her translation favourably to that of Murray: 'Gilbert Murray has struck at Greek scholarship and done no good to English verse,' but 'H.D. is a poet . . . she has turned Euripides into English verse which can be taken seriously, verse of our own time.' Unlike Murray, 'she does succeed in bringing something out of the Greek language to the English,' Eliot concluded, 'in an immediate contact which gives life to both, the contact which makes it possible for the modern language perpetually to draw sustenance from the dead'.[35]

In February 1916, the Aldingtons moved to Mecklenburgh Square in Bloomsbury. 'A most beautiful dilapidated old square', Eliot described it after a visit there, 'a square in the middle of town, near King's Cross Station, but with spacious old gardens about it'.[36] But they sublet the property almost immediately in order to live in the countryside in North Devon, where they enjoyed a rustic life of long hikes in the snow, chopping firewood, witnessing the arrival of spring flowers, skinny-dipping, making marmalade and, of course, writing and translating. The Military Service Act of 1916, however, would change their lives irrevocably. The controversial Act divided the Liberal Party and caused the Home Secretary, Sir John Simon, to resign. Hundreds of thousands of Londoners filled Trafalgar Square in protest, to no avail. The British military needed more men in the trenches. On average, 5,000 men per day were dying on the Western front – totalling 100,000 casualties in 1914 and 1915. Facing a German army double their size, the British had no choice but to retreat from their first engagement. Richard had tried, and failed, to enter officers' training pre-emptively.[37] When conscription of married men began in May 1916, Richard and his friend Carl Fallas, anticipating the inevitable, voluntarily enlisted.

Richard's enlistment came at a difficult moment in his marriage, for their relationship had not fully recovered from Richard's affair with Carl's wife, Flo, that spring. About the affair, H.D.'s position seems to have been that Richard's dalliance was permissible as long as it inspired him creatively: 'life is made for beautiful love', she wrote in 'Amaranth', 'let him take beauty/ as his right.' But that did not mean that she wasn't terribly hurt, especially after discovering in print two candid love poems for Flo that Richard had not shared with her. 'How I hate you for this,' she expressed her bitterness in response, 'was my beauty so slight a gift,/ so soon, so soon forgot?' She transformed her agony into

Richard Aldington, in uniform, 1918.

poetry, trauma becoming her inspiration: 'to sing love,/ love must first shatter us.'[38]

Still, the two remained committed to their marriage. H.D. moved to Corfe Castle from Parracombe to be closer to Richard's training camp in Wareham, and then later to Lichfield, near Birmingham, when he was transferred. She even offered to bring Flo to Corfe Castle. Their most intense point of disagreement that year concerned whether or not H.D. should return to the States now that Richard was a soldier. Richard felt that she must leave, reasoning, 'If I die when Hilda is in America, she will feel it less.'[39] While she wavered in the autumn of 1916 after a brief illness, by the end of the year her resolve to stay in England was firm. When Flint interceded on her behalf, Richard retorted: 'If she wants to stay, she stays; whatever happens later is not my fault. The responsibility will be with her – and her advisers! . . . what I have done has been only an attempt to minimise the shock to the person I love most.'[40] A few days later, he added, with rare bitterness toward his then closest friend, 'I don't mind betting that all women under 30 without children are industrially conscripted within 6 months . . . If H.D. *is* industrially conscripted I shall never forgive you people who have persuaded her to stay.'[41] Staying was not without its challenges. Fletcher recalls that 'H.D. was, most of the time, too distraught by the War and by the prospect of losing Aldington to provide good company.'[42]

While Richard was in training camps, H.D. was busy working on *The Egoist*, where she was to take Richard's editorial role from 1 June 1916 until 1 June 1917, when T. S. Eliot assumed the position. As editor, she followed in the tradition of Pound and Aldington by publishing her own work, but she also got several unknown American poets into print, and published poetry by Pound, Flint, D. H. Lawrence, Yone Noguchi and May Sinclair. Essays by Aldington, their close friend John Cournos and William Carlos Williams also appeared in volumes under her editorial direction. Perhaps most importantly, she published verse by Marianne Moore long before she became well known – Moore's first published poem, in fact, had appeared in *The Egoist* – and penned a laudatory review of her work:

> with all the assurance of the perfect swordsman, the perfect technician, Miss Moore turns her perfect craft as the perfect craftsman must inevitably do, to some direct presentation

To
Marianne Moore
H.D.

H.D., early 1920s.

of beauty, clear, cut in flowing lines . . . frail, yet as all beautiful things are, absolutely hard – and destined to endure longer, far longer than the toppling sky-scrapers, and the world of shrapnel and machine-guns in which we live.[43]

H.D. could have been describing her own work. She and Moore, who would go on to edit *The Dial*, would continue to advocate for one another's writings throughout their lives.

Aldington was finally sent to France in December of 1916, on the heels of the end of the bloody Battle of the Somme, fought in large part by civilian volunteers and which had taken the lives of 125,000 British men. His outlook was bleak, as was hers. She cheered the American entrance into the war in April of the following year, but it did little to allay her fears. The war was beginning to seem interminable, and Aldington grew more and more depressed, convinced that he would die in battle.

After a month of combat, Richard encouraged Flint to find H.D., 'a grass widow', an '"*affaire*" *pour passer le temps*'.[44] In fact, H.D. had begun an open flirtation on the day that Aldington left for training camp, with John Cournos, a Ukrainian-born Jewish writer and translator who had grown up in Philadelphia. Cournos met H.D. through Pound, and he was one of their circle throughout the war years. He was with H.D. and Richard that night in 1914 outside Buckingham Palace, and he lived first in Ezra's Church Walk flat and then at Mecklenburgh Square, visiting the Aldingtons frequently in North Devon. He found the couple, who lived and worked in tandem, an ideal model for a marriage.[45]

Over time, Cournos's fondness for H.D. deepened, and after an impulsive kiss the day Aldington left for the front, he fell for her. H.D. felt that Cournos shared her spiritual and aesthetic values, and with Richard absent – emotionally, and now physically – she needed a muse. But she was dedicated to the idea that art was to be prioritized above life – that life was the very substance of art – and this belief guided both her response to Aldington's infidelity and her chaste romancing of Cournos. 'When I said I could love you . . . I meant if it would help R[ichard],' she explained when he urged her to leave her husband. 'If being torn by unanswered passion is going to make R. a great poet, we must not let *any* personal consideration come between R. and his work.' What matters more than emotion is the art that flows from it: 'The hurt I suffered has freed my song – this is most precious to me . . . to deny *love* entrance is to crush and break beauty.'[46] Likewise, if being in love with H.D. inspired Cournos to create, then that love was to be cultivated, though not consummated: 'I had a feeling that I might help you with your work – that your affection for me might at any rate.'[47]

Complicating the matter further was Cournos's on-again, off-again engagement to another Philadelphian, Dorothy 'Arabella' Yorke, a young art student, who did not return his affections even as she heartlessly encouraged them – she told Cournos's stepson many years later, 'I never really loved John; I only pitied him.'[48] In the autumn of 1917, at Cournos's request, Yorke was living at the Aldingtons' flat at Mecklenburgh Square. By the end of that year, Richard commenced an affair with her, during his leaves from the Front, that would last a decade. It haunted H.D. into her old age, as she wrote and rewrote the story in the years to come. Cournos quickly forgave Richard and Arabella, placing the blame, instead, solely on H.D., whom he 'came to hate . . . implacably', feelings that had not abated even decades later, in 1960, when she published *Bid Me to Live* about the Mecklenburgh Square imbroglios of the war years.[49]

The Aldingtons, the Pounds and their expansive circles moved constantly in the 1910s, leasing and subleasing one another's homes. In *Bid Me to Live*, she describes the peripatetic lifestyle of the young moderns: 'they found themselves in out-of-the-way cottages, in a room in Kensington, in two rooms in Hampstead, in a huge drawing-room in Bloomsbury. So-and-so knows someone who has a cottage; won't you take it . . .? . . . Take so-and-so's cottage

. . . a sort of lodge I believe.'[50] The Aldingtons' Bloomsbury flat became temporary quarters for a number of their friends during the First World War, including D. H. and Frieda Lawrence. Frieda, a German, had left her husband and children for Lawrence; the two were under suspicion during the war, as adulterers and German spies. When the Lawrences could not find anyone willing to rent lodgings to them, H.D. offered refuge. H.D. and Richard had befriended Lawrence as a fellow Imagist, advocating strongly for his inclusion in the *Some Imagist Poets* series – overruling Lowell, who viewed him as a scandalous figure whose poetry might draw obscenity charges and mar the Imagist brand.[51] For a time, H.D. and Lawrence were close, exchanging and workshopping their poems and his novel *Women in Love*.

Fletcher remembered Lawrence as 'spare, gnarled, peasantlike, with [a] fiery beard and intense vitality'.[52] While he was gaunt and prone to illness, Lawrence nonetheless exuded an alluring energy. On occasions when Richard was granted leave, H.D. convened everyone to celebrate, an event often involving staged readings and performances. Some years later, Brigit Patmore set the scene of the vibrant personalities of this Bloomsbury ensemble (absent Cournos, who had been sent by the Foreign Office to Russia):

In the Aldingtons' room the apricot-coloured walls were lit by candles, dark blue curtains covered the windows. A table had a large red platter heaped with fruit, and a huge plate held whatever could be got of ham and sausages, and there was bread and wine. Everyone burned with a different incandescence. Frieda in a sun-drenched way, wild, blonde hair waving happily, grey-green eyes raying out laughter, her fair skin an effulgent pale rose. Lorenzo [Lawrence], as if he had drunk fire and was quite used to it. Hilda, a swaying sapling almost destroyed by tempests, all the blueness of flame gone into her large distracted eyes. Cecil Gray was a shaded candle, he held his intelligence watchfully behind spectacles. Arabella, the only dark one amongst us, smouldered under her polished hair . . . Richard flickered with the desperate gaiety of the soldier on leave and unresolved pain.[53]

H.D. and Lawrence did not have a sexual relationship, despite speculation to the contrary. But for a short time, they felt spiritually connected through their work. It was rare for H.D. to end a friendship – 'I am loyal literally to death,' she acknowledged in a questionnaire in the *Little Review*[54] – but in *Bid Me to Live*, she characterizes their parting as the result of a debate over gender that could not be resolved. Her protagonist, Julia, is the recipient of sharp criticism from Rico (based on Lawrence) when she shares with him an Orpheus sequence: 'How can you know what Orpheus feels?' he demands, 'It's your part to be woman, the woman vibration.'[55] But Julia rejects his stance as wrong-headed and outmoded: 'That was not true. This mood, this realm of consciousness was sexless, or all sex . . . This man-, this woman-theory of Rico's was false, it creaked in the joints.'[56] Lawrence, 'for all of his acceptance of her verses, had shouted his man-is-man, his woman-is-woman at her; his shrill peacock-cry sounded a love-cry, death-cry for their generation'. The two, Julia realizes, were merely useful to one another as inspiration – catalysts in a laboratory 'experiment', 'acid' in a 'seething test-tube' – so when his commentary on her work was impossibly inflected through misogyny, he ceased to be useful or interesting to her, and their bond was broken: 'The fireworks had sizzled out, the show was over.'[57] On that point at least, they were in accord. His final letter to her read, 'I hope never to see you again.'[58]

The quiet 'shaded candle' of the group, Cecil Gray, was a Scottish composer and music critic, nearly a decade younger than H.D., whom, as Arabella began to occupy all of Richard's leave time, Gray wooed, initially quite passionately. In her autobiographical novel

Asphodel, he is christened, tellingly, Cyril Vane – Vanio in *Bid Me to Live*. He is 'young, wealthy', 'Etruscan with his thin face', 'tall and gentle and not heavy and not domineering like her husband'.[59] When Cyril invites Hermione (based on H.D.) to live and work with him in Cornwall, her husband acquiesces. Lonely and depressed, Hermione sees an opportunity to escape the increasingly claustrophobic atmosphere of Mecklenburgh Square, where she shares rooms with her husband's paramour and bears witness to their trysts; in real life, Richard and Arabella were so public in their lovemaking that the landlady complained to H.D. that she felt morally compromised.[60] In March 1918, H.D. joined Gray in Zennor, near Bosigran Castle, a coastal fort on a granite cliff dating from the Iron Age.

H.D. and Gray lived in a Cornwall home that Lawrence called haunted, and she reported seeing ghosts there.[61] She was productive, working on new poetry and translations, just as she had been at other abodes outside of London. This migratory pattern was one that would set the rhythm for much of the rest of her life: moving away from the hustle and bustle of London life in order to concentrate solely on writing, then plunging back into the fray for stimulation and inspiration. In *Bid Me to Live*, Cornwall proves to be a uniquely apt setting for translation work: 'The Greek words went with the texture of the stones here,' her narrator is thrilled to learn. Indeed, H.D.'s view of translation in this period is more tactile than visual: 'She was like one blind, reading the texture of incised letters, rejoicing like one blind who knows an inner light . . . Anyone can translate the meaning of the word. She wanted the shape, the feel of it, the character of it.'[62]

The two spent the summer together, before parting ways for good in August when H.D. learned she was pregnant. If we are to take *Asphodel* as our guide, Gray did not react well to the announcement that H.D. was carrying their child. In the novel, he stiffly offers to marry her, and she wisely refuses his reluctant proposal. In real life, H.D. vacated Mecklenburgh Square the same month that she left Gray, moving to the wooded countryside of Speen in Buckinghamshire, northwest of London. There she shared a cottage with a girlhood friend – Margaret Snively Pratt, whose British husband was away at the Front – next door to another friend, the newspaper editor Clement Shorter. H.D. proceeded cautiously through her second pregnancy, ever mindful of the tragedy of her first.

Throughout her time with Gray, she and Richard had been writing to one another as regularly as they always had. Their physical encounters, too, in early 1918, had become increasingly passionate. Aldington felt genuinely torn between his love for Hilda and his lust for Arabella: 'I love you and I desire – *l'autre*', he professed to H.D. in May of 1918.[63] He was depressed, his mood erratic. In the space of just a few days, he told Cournos that he was in love with Arabella, and Flint that he and Arabella were just having fun. To Flint, he affirmed, '[H.D. and I] are "parted" to the extent that I am in France and she in Cornwall. But we are not "parted" in any other sense. We write each other, *comme toujours*. You – *et le monde* – are very blind if you think anything could ever part us two.'[64] 'I am tenderly and passionately in love with you,' he reassured H.D. in July.[65] He had told her he would get over her fling with Gray, but upon learning of her pregnancy, Richard ultimately made a decision that would prove to be final. They would be friends and colleagues, but they would never live together again.

In many ways, their marriage was a war casualty. 'The war was my husband,' she recalled in the year before she died.[66] Aldington was transformed by his military service. He would never regain the idealism of his youth. In his novel about the war, *Death of a Hero*, he depicts battle as 'a timeless confusion, a chaos of noise, fatigue, anxiety, and horror'.[67] 'His personal life became intolerable because of the War,' his narrator observes, 'and the War became intolerable because of his own life.'[68] The narrator feels empty, evacuated of humanity – a 'murder-robot' – and he ends his own life on the

H.D. and Perdita.

battlefield.[69] In her own autobiographical fiction about the period, H.D. reflects on her cohort as not a 'lost generation' but a 'war-generation', as 'a curious race' who 'lived before the black cloud fell'.[70] Her husband was scarcely recognizable, not her husband but 'this person that came back to her, with the smell of gas in his breath, with the stench of death in his clothes'. A non-combatant, she, too, felt empty: '[The war] shut her out from life . . . out of touch with all humanity.'[71]

The First World War had ended, but 1918 and 1919 were nonetheless years of great turmoil, and not just because of H.D.'s separation from Richard. Her brother Gilbert was killed in action in France on 25 September 1918, less than two months before the war ended, and this brought on, H.D. believed, the death of her father just six months later. Moreover, the pregnancy was, again, not an easy one. Late in her third trimester, she contracted the pandemic influenza of 1918. Of avian origins, the flu strain infected 500 million people, or one-third of the world's population, killing 50–100 million. It has been called the most deadly epidemic in recorded global history, and H.D. was gravely ill for a time, not expected to live. But at St Faith's Nursing Home for Gentlepeople in Ealing, ailing from double pneumonia, H.D. gave birth to Frances Perdita on the last day of March 1919, naming her for Frances Gregg and for Hermione's daughter in Shakespeare's *The Winter's Tale*, because, as 'daffodils that come before the swallow dares', she 'takes the winds of March with beauty'.[72] Oscillating between proclamations of support and reversals, Aldington threatened her with legal action if she registered her daughter in his name. She did so anyway.

H.D. had decided that raising a child alone would be preferable to raising one with Aldington or Gray. In *Asphodel*, Hermione associates men with the violence of the war, not with the tenderness of parenthood. 'Must she go back to men, men, men?' she asks herself, 'She was stronger than men, men, men – she was stronger than guns, guns, guns.'[73] Those tumultuous years at war's end also brought a new love into H.D.'s life, Winifred 'Bryher' Ellerman, who was to become her lifelong partner. She would not have to raise Perdita alone. Perdita would have two mothers.

4

'to make a self', 1919–26

It was love at first sight for Bryher. In her writings, she described H.D. as 'spear flower if a spear could bloom', with 'eyes that had the sea in them, the fire and colour and the splendour of it'.[1] 'I had a friend at last who talked to me about poetry and did not laugh at my meagre attempts at writing,' she recalled decades later, 'and H.D. was the most beautiful figure that I have ever seen in my life, with a face that came directly from a Greek statue and, almost to the end, the body of an athlete.'[2] H.D. adjudged Bryher 'an extremely pretty creature'.[3] She was, as she had been with Frances, drawn to Bryher's eyes, 'too intense for this generation': 'she knew she would never, never escape those eyes that looked and looked and looked.'[4] There was undeniable lust. But it was not love at first sight for H.D.

Bryher and H.D. were an unlikely couple: one was a middle-class American, a published and acclaimed poet, a woman who had lived and loved and survived many personal traumas; the other an extravagantly wealthy British heiress who, eight years H.D.'s junior, had dreams but little life experience. H.D. depended on ritual and solitude, Bryher on constant activity and travel. H.D. was sensitive to noise; Bryher was oblivious to the clamour and ruckus that seemed ever to accompany her. H.D. needed freedom, Bryher a sense of control. 'You are limited in your outlook,' H.D.'s autobiographically based protagonist of *Paint It Today* complains to Althea (based on Bryher). 'I do not understand your philosophy,'

Althea counters. 'Our worlds are worlds apart,' Althea insists. 'Our worlds are not so many worlds apart' is the retort.[5] H.D.'s feelings took time to develop. At one point, H.D. confided to Cournos that Bryher's intensity troubled her: 'the girl is in love with me, so madly that it is terrible. No man has ever cared for me like that.'[6]

Discovering that Bryher and Frances Gregg shared a birthday – 2 September – would have hinted at a shared destiny for H.D., an amateur astrologer. On that date in 1894, Bryher was born Annie Winifred E. Glover in Kent to Hannah Glover and John Ellerman, who was to become the richest man in England. They lived together as a family, but it was not until Hannah was expecting a son – John, born in 1909 – that she married Bryher's father. An accountant by training, Ellerman amassed a fortune of £37 million (around £3.1 billion by today's standards) by investing in breweries, ships and aristocratic real estate, and by buying up and flipping under-priced companies. By all accounts, Ellerman was devoted to the striking Glover, to the point of alarming fits of jealousy: she was, in her own chilling words, preserved 'in a glass case'.[7] Perhaps due to his controlling nature, or perhaps due to his vast fortune, the family led 'a frighteningly anti-social and lonely life'.[8] Bryher was raised in Sussex, London and abroad: Egypt, Italy, Spain, Algeria, Tunisia, Switzerland. She did not attend school until, as a young teen, she was sent to Queenswood Boarding School as a day student so that she could learn to acclimate to others her age.[9] She hated it. The world of Bryher's childhood was, in its way, as insular as that of H.D.'s.

Bryher's early childhood was marred by a singular source of great disappointment: 'Her one regret was that she was a girl.'[10] On this point, she never changed her mind. She was 'Two selves. Jammed against each other, disjointed and ill-fitting,' one a girl and one a boy.[11] She wanted to wear boy's clothing, to eat hearty English food, to run away to the sea and work on a ship, to live – in short – a life of 'unrestricted freedom. Be a girl and there were

Bryher, from the H.D. scrapbook.

always barriers.'[12] 'If she had been a boy life would have lain at her feet,' she thought.[13] While she wanted to associate only with boys, they held no erotic interest for her. Today she may have identified as queer or transgender, but in the Victorian and Edwardian periods, no such possibilities existed. To make matters worse, she wanted to be a writer, an artist and an intellectual, dreams her parents were determined to quash. When she met the famous anthropologist Margaret Murray while taking classes in Arabic, she was offered the opportunity to train in archaeology with her, but her parents vowed to pull her out of lessons and keep her at home.[14] 'My family was truly frightened', she recalled in a later memoir, 'of the free-thinking little monster that had emerged in their midst.'[15] By the end of the First World War, Bryher was in despair over what looked to be a hopeless future.

Meeting H.D., then, was revelatory and, for both, in a very real sense, life-saving – Bryher was suicidal, and H.D. nearly died from the 1918–19 influenza before Bryher got her access to better medical care. Bryher was already a devotee when she met H.D., having discovered *Des Imagistes* in 1914, devouring it 'with the lusty, roaring appetite of an Elizabethan boy'.[16] She had been writing poetry herself for several years, and somehow convinced her father to fund a book of her own verse, *The Region of Lutany*, in 1914. A fan letter to Amy Lowell in 1918 yielded a copy of H.D.'s *Sea Garden*, which she read and reread until she knew it by heart. At last, she wrote to H.D., who invited her to tea at Bosigran Castle, where she was living with Cecil Gray. The day – 17 July 1918 – was enshrined, an anniversary the two would celebrate the rest of their lives.

After Perdita's birth, H.D. attempted to establish boundaries, which Bryher merely pretended to abide. With Perdita tucked away at the exclusive 'Babies' Hotel' of the Norland Nurseries, H.D., still recovering from illness, settled in Kensington nearby so that she could see her daughter daily. Bryher began making a frenzy of travel plans for them. H.D. was cautious, reluctant to

leave Perdita but lured by the prospects Bryher laid before her:
'I am torn between a desire for a little place with Perdita and fairy-
books and Noahs arks and dolls, and a wild adventure.'[17] Bryher
persisted. Their first trip was close to home: Bryher wanted H.D.
to see the Scilly Islands, where she had discovered her name one
summer with one of her only school friends, Doris Banfield. H.D.
and Bryher's expedition in the summer of 1919 inspired H.D.'s
aesthetic manifesto, *Notes on Thought and Vision*. In the Scillys,
H.D. had her '"jelly-fish" experience'.[18] Hypothesizing a state
beyond body and mind called 'over-mind', H.D. describes a
translucent 'cap of consciousness' with jellyfish tentacles creating
a network of sensation across the body.[19] Artists, she avers, must
indulge in the pleasures of the body, the mind and over-mind.
Vision of the womb and vision of the brain alike determine artistic
consciousness. Thus, one must develop one's physicality and
sexuality, not just one's intellect or sense of aesthetics: 'We must be
"in love" before we can understand the mysteries of vision.' 'There
is no great art period,' she asserts, 'without great lovers.'[20]

The next trip, highly anticipated, was to Greece – the site of
so much of H.D.'s writing. The two were accompanied by the
sexologist Havelock Ellis, who, with John Addington Symonds, had
written *Sexual Inversion* in 1900, which discussed homosexuality
without reference to immorality or illness. Ellis's wife, Edith Lees,
was an outspoken suffragette and lesbian. Intrigued by her friend
Daphne Bax's depiction of Ellis as 'a recluse, a Titan, a giant', H.D.
had gone to see him in Brixton: 'I had expected to meet the rather
remote, detached, and much-abused scientist, I found the artist.'[21]
After reading the manuscript of Bryher's autobiographical novel
Development, H.D. shared it with Ellis, who agreed to see Bryher in
February of 1919. When Ellis reassured her that 'she was only a girl
by accident,' Bryher was grateful.[22] (She would be pleased when
a later psychoanalyst told her that her 'eroticism is that of male –
sugar to the tail'.[23]) The three set sail from London on 7 February

1920, and arrived in Greece by the end of the month. Ellis left in March, but Bryher and H.D. toured the Greek Isles after a month-long stay in Athens.

H.D. had three mystical experiences on that trip, experiences that were to resurface in her writing and her dreams for years to come. En route to Greece, aboard ss *Borodino*, H.D. met middle-aged architect and archaeologist Pieter Rodeck on deck, then later discovered that he had been below deck at the time. The imagined encounter haunted H.D., and she later interpreted the episode as an instance of 'bi-location': 'It is a mystery not uncommon to folk and fairy-tales, the mystery of the appearance of a stranger or a near-stranger, at a time and in a place where he could not possibly have been.'[24]

The other two mystical experiences occurred in Corfu, where H.D. was blissful amidst the 'flowers, spring, orange trees, lead-pencil cypresses' of the island.[25] Site of the marriage of Jason and Medea, Corfu is rich in mythological and historical significance, and H.D. and Bryher explored its temples and archaeological sites. One evening in their hotel room, H.D. went into a mediumistic trance while enacting a series of *tableaux vivants* and dances for Bryher. Recounting the experience in an autobiographical novel, *Majic Ring*, H.D. describes how she shifted from *performing* a range of historical figures across the globe to *becoming* them, possessing their bodies and viewing their worlds through their eyes.

The second of these Corfu visions was shared by H.D. and Bryher. On the bedroom wall, the two glimpsed in 'a sort of halfway state between ordinary dream and the vision of those who . . . we must call psychics or clairvoyants' a series of 'shadow' or 'light-pictures'. The first was 'a stencil or stamp of a soldier or airman' that seemed familiar to her, a 'dead brother? lost friend?' The second was a goblet or cup, the third reminiscent of 'the tripod of classic Delphi . . . venerated object of the cult of the sun god', with people swarming beneath it. H.D. perceived a fourth image drawn on the wall – an image of Niké, goddess of victory – then Bryher saw a sun disc and an artist appear.[26] Sigmund Freud later diagnosed the vision as 'a desire for union with [her] mother', but H.D. characterized it as 'merely an extension of the artist's mind, a *picture* or an illustrated poem, taken out of the actual dream or daydream content and projected from within'.[27] And as a chilling harbinger of another great war to come.

The following year, a third international trip was undertaken. For Bryher, the United States had always stood as a beacon of freedom: in America, 'Girls had jobs!' H.D. gamely attempted to warn her that the United States would not live up to her unrealistic expectations, but for Bryher, America was her 'first love affair'.[28] If 'England stinks of history', America would be the antidote, she was convinced.[29] Forbidden by her parents to go unchaperoned, she would at long last cross the Atlantic in September of 1920 on the luxury liner ss *Adriatic* with H.D. and Perdita in tow. With an inflated sense of optimism, they listed the United States as their intended country of future residence on ship documents. Landing briefly in New York – during which time they saw Marianne Moore and her mother, Amy Lowell and her partner Ada – they proceeded to California, the outermost point of Bryher's mythological West. Unhappy in Santa Barbara, they settled in Carmel for the autumn and much of the winter, where H.D. worked on a series of essays on the Greek poets and dramatists Euripides, Pausanias, Meleager, Theocritus, Anacreon and Sappho.

When H.D. was not working, she and Bryher romped in the woods, taking nude photographs of one another. Ultimately, however, America was a bitter disappointment to Bryher, proving every bit as fusty, provincial and conventional as England, even as the sublimity of its utterly alien landscapes – its untrodden forests and red-rock-studded deserts – overwhelmed and frightened her. 'Here was a different civilization,' she remarked in the *roman-à-clef West*, 'beautiful, brutal, incredibly destructive.'[30] But Bryher was

H.D., California, 1920, from the H.D. scrapbook.

steadfast that she would not submit to the stultifying existence at her parents' mansion on South Audley Street. She would not leave behind her American freedom. On Valentine's Day of 1921, she married a bisexual American writer, Robert McAlmon, whom she had met in New York only a few months earlier. Now an American citizen and a married woman, Bryher returned to a life in England that would not be governed so firmly by her parents' wishes.

Back in Europe, they rarely stayed in one place. McAlmon hated London and promptly relocated to Paris. H.D. had long been more productive when she could alternate between quiet and lively locations. Bryher was eager to make a new home in Switzerland, outside of her parents' reach. A pattern of migration between London and Switzerland was established (with sojourns in Paris and Italy) that would prove a model to which they adhered until the outbreak of the Second World War. Plunging into London life for several months at a time, H.D. wrote daily, but also found time to see friends, indulge in flirtations and affairs with men and women and immerse herself in the city's museums and nightlife. Tiring of the whirlwind, she would then isolate herself in Bryher's flat in the Swiss Alps for long, more intensive periods of writing. 'While not homeless,' Annette Debo has astutely observed, 'H.D. was placeless.'[31]

For several years H.D.'s mother, and for a period her Aunt Laura, lived with them, helping with childcare so that H.D. and Bryher could have time and space to work. The 1920s were perhaps H.D.'s most productive decade, rivalled only by the explosion of writing of the 1940s, inspired by the war. But it took time for the two to adjust to life together. Like Bryher, H.D. was frugal, but H.D. was decidedly unimpressed with the extravagance of the Ellermans' home life. Bryher was used to having a staff of servants, while H.D., with obsessive-compulsive tendencies, preferred keeping her own house.[32] H.D. would enjoy the benefits of Bryher's bank account, but she could have just as well existed without it, having previously subsisted comfortably on a modest sum provided by her father in the 1910s. A more serious difference between them involved their relationship to London. Like her husband, Bryher wished to spend as little time there as possible, while H.D. idealized it as the city that had welcomed her nascent literary pursuits after her escape from America, and all of her friends were there. But Bryher had her parents to contend with. Even after she married, when in London, Bryher kept secret H.D.'s and Perdita's presence just a mile away from the Ellerman estate, 'in a small service flat, sharing a bedroom'. Perdita remembers Bryher as 'haunted and hunted' on stolen visits.[33]

H.D. considered London her home and did not share Bryher's love for Switzerland – she found it 'expensive and grandiose . . . no tradition and yet something . . . putrid underneath'.[34] She chafed at being stuck too long in *Suisse* (as they called it). In 1922 and 1923, H.D. lived in Florence and Capri for the best part of a year, trying, without success, to convince Bryher to relocate. Neither wanted Perdita to be educated in England, but once the girl was old enough to travel easily, H.D. grew more emphatic. In 1924, Bryher bribed her with kittens, but in 1925, H.D. put her foot down and Bryher relented. They relocated to London for a year; however, it was so damaging to Bryher to live in such close proximity to her parents that they returned to a migratory life the following year. H.D. was willing to accept a Swiss home, provided she could keep a permanent London flat. Though she preferred Bloomsbury, she settled on one in Kensington, across the street from the McAlmons, where Bob, on the rare instances when he was in town to perform the role of dutiful spouse to his in-laws, threw 'wild parties'.[35]

London and Paris, in the years that H.D. and Bryher spent in the cities in the 1920s – a decade bookended by a demoralizing world war and the devastating Great Depression – were oases. The early 1920s was a time of idealism and opulence, despite (or, likely, because of) the economic impact of the First World War on both cities. Women bobbed their hair, scandalously shortened their skirts, obtained birth control, dabbled in bisexuality and smoked and drank in jazz clubs, music halls and cabarets. H.D. and Bryher abandoned corsets and petticoats for loose tunics and even trousers. Bryher's attire became more and more masculine as the decade progressed. H.D. had already cut her long hair and sported a modishly severe fringe. She was never fond of alcohol, but she smoked zealously.

The 1920s were the heyday of literary modernism, seeing the publication of T. S. Eliot's *The Waste Land*, Virginia Woolf's *To the Lighthouse* and *Mrs Dalloway*, D. H. Lawrence's salacious *Lady Chatterley's Lover*, William Carlos Williams's *Spring and All*, Ernest Hemingway's *The Sun Also Rises*, Bertolt Brecht's *The Threepenny Opera*, Marianne Moore's *Observations*, James Joyce's *Ulysses*, Gertrude Stein's *The Making of Americans*, William Faulkner's *The Sound and the Fury*, E. M. Forster's *A Passage to India*, Ezra Pound's *The Cantos* and Eugene O'Neill's *Desire Under the Elms*. A nearly

H.D., 1920s.

nude Josephine Baker titillated Parisian nightclub audiences, while Londoners flocked to theatres to see Noël Coward plays. The Harlem Renaissance in the United States exposed audiences to African American novels like Jean Toomer's *Cane* and Nella Larsen's *Quicksand*, and poetry by Langston Hughes and Claude McKay.

In this period, H.D. and (especially) Bryher encountered nearly everybody who was anybody in the literary–artistic worlds of Paris and London, which harboured as many Americans as Europeans. Bryher was naturally shy – her unusual childhood left her unaccustomed to navigating social settings – but McAlmon was a born networker, and of course everyone was anxious to meet a wealthy lover of the arts. Bryher's letters to H.D. about a trip to Paris are filled with gossip about encounters with Nora Joyce (James Joyce's wife), the Hemingways (with whom she dined), the Pounds, Man Ray and Kiki (from whom she received impromptu photography lessons), Djuna Barnes and Thelma Wood (they're happy together, she reported), Mary Butts (usually drunk), Stein and Alice B. Toklas and a host of other modernist luminaries. H.D. still saw the Pounds frequently, but her and Bryher's circle widened considerably to include such figures as Shakespeare & Co. bookshop proprietors Sylvia Beach and Adrienne Monnier, heiress and activist Nancy Cunard, novelist Norman Douglas, the denizens of Natalie Barney's famed Sapphic salon, writer and activist Kay Boyle, playwright Thornton Wilder, Cecil Maitland and Mary Butts (whose lurid fiction was eagerly consumed and circulated between them whenever it appeared in print), novelist Dorothy Richardson, artists Constantin Brancusi and Man Ray (who photographed both women), and of course Gertrude Stein and her assembly of Continental artists.

These connections were mutually beneficial. In the 1920s, Bryher established herself as a formidable patron of modernism. With Bryher's funds, McAlmon established Contact Press in Paris in 1922 and (with William Carlos Williams) the little magazine

H.D. by Man Ray, 1922, Paris.

Contact. Contact Press made a significant impact on modernism, publishing work by Ezra Pound, Gertrude Stein, Ernest Hemingway, Djuna Barnes, Ford Madox Ford and H. D. McAlmon. Bryher, too, helped support James Joyce while he was writing *Ulysses*, and their friend Sylvia Beach famously had it printed. With H.D.'s help, Bryher surprised Marianne Moore with the publication of Moore's first book of poems in 1921, a surprise that was not altogether welcome. It damaged Moore's relationship with both women, though she was, as Annette Debo notes, more open with Bryher about 'her shock, her anger, and her alarm'.[36]

H.D. and Bryher lived, worked and travelled together, and they wrote poetry to one another. Published in *Poetry* in 1920, Bryher's three-part 'Hellenics' is a testament to her love for H.D.: thanking Aphrodite 'that at last my body is at peace', the speaker revels in 'The hollows under your knees . . . sweet with love', the 'April scent of your throat' and the 'soft white petals of your feet'. These poems of adoration are sexually explicit: 'Under your lifted arm/ There is lavender to kiss;/ Sea-lavender, spiced with salt', the speaker gushes as she 'touch[es] the pansy set below your heart'. 'Your face is Greece,' she declares, 'I have only the fire of my heart to offer you.'[37]

H.D.'s 'Halcyon' (originally 'Grey Gull') was written for their seventh anniversary. 'Why am I vague, unsure,' the speaker asks,

> until you are blown,
> unexpected, small, quaint, unnoticeable,
> a grey gull,
> into a room.

H.D. was not sentimental. The small 'unconscionable little gull', she laments, has been 'sent . . . to shatter my peace'.[38] But while she testifies to their 'quarrels' – noting Bryher's tendency toward being 'bitter and crude to me' – she nonetheless maintains that without her, she was 'a bird with a broken wing', dwelling in 'something like a desert apart/ without hope of oasis'.[39] 'O for you,' she sings in tribute, 'now life will begin/ all over again', 'for you – for ever –/ mysterious little gull'.[40]

H.D. dedicated her next book of poetry, *Hymen* (1921), to Bryher and Perdita. 'If *Sea Garden* represents Innocence,' the poet Alicia Ostriker has observed, 'the postwar poetry represents Experience.'[41]

Set, as her previous books, in ancient Greece, *Hymen* is filled with mothers and daughters coming of age, deceptive men and scorned lovers, remnants of H.D.'s arduous late war years – many of the poems were drafted during her difficult pregnancy. The poems of this volume give voice to female Greek mythological characters: an angry 'Demeter', who has lost her daughter to marriage; 'Simaetha', bitter over her neglectful lover; Achilles' mother 'Thetis' in the moment before her loss of innocence; 'Leda' after the rape; a scorned 'Circe' after Ulysses' departure; the deserted 'Evadne'.

But there are also poems that express boundless optimism about love, and hope for the future, as William Carlos Williams noted in an unpublished review that deemed 'Simaetha' and 'Circe' 'not surpassed in American letters'.[42] 'The whole white world is ours,' the speaker exclaims in one such poem of *Hymen*,

> ours is the wind-breath
> at the hot noon-hour,
> ours is the bee's soft belly
> and the blush of the rose-petal,
> lifted, of the flower.[43]

'The "whole white world", it seems, is not an empirical but an erotic entity,' Eileen Gregory explains: 'The whiteness here . . . does not refer to light or color in itself but to a sensuous consummation.'[44] 'Can honey distill such fragrance/ as your bright hair?' the speaker asks in 'Song',

> for your face is as fair as rain,
> yet as rain that lies clear
> on white honey-comb,
> lends radiance to the white wax,
> so your hair on your brow
> casts light for a shadow.[45]

A translation of Sappho gives us

> heat, more passionate
> of bone and the white shell
> and fiery tempered steel.[46]

Hymen's titular poem stages a procession of a virgin to her lover on their wedding night. Though often read as rape – as 'an act of rapture that is also an act of rupture'[47] – the poem is remarkable, like the better-known 'Leda', for its eroticism and absence of violence. 'Love', the bridegroom, is a bee with 'honey-seeking lips', who 'clings close and warmly sips,/ And seeks with honey-thighs to sway/ And drink the very flower away'. Only after cunnilingus deflowers the bride does 'the plunderer slip/ Between the purple flower-lips'.[48] When she sent 'Hymen' to *Poetry*, she anticipated 'a lecture . . . on my Asiatic abandon!' from its editor, Harriet Monroe.[49] She must have been surprised that May Sinclair, several years later, found 'austere ecstasy' in this volume. Ever fascinated by H.D., Sinclair would declare *Hymen*'s poems 'perfect things' of 'strange new beauty', pointedly disagreeing with an abysmal review in *The Times*.[50] Marianne Moore reviewed the book in *Broom* in 1923, depicting H.D.'s work as 'life denuded of subterfuge', the 'clean violence of truth'.[51]

Wherever she went, H.D. brought pictures of Bryher and Perdita to place on her 'altar'. Letters between H.D. and Bryher in the 1920s reveal a relationship that was warm, playfully erotic and flirtatious. When apart – rare in the early to mid-1920s – they sent letters to one another daily. Following, perhaps, Marianne Moore's practice, they imparted nicknames to one another, often animal names, adding sketches and 'paw prints' to their signatures. H.D. calls Bryher 'Boy' or the canine 'Fido', and Bryher dubs H.D. 'Horse', or, alternatively, 'Unicorn' or 'Puma'. Anticipating Bryher's return from Paris in a letter of spring 1924, H.D. seductively entices her: 'I will comfort you and buy some green corsets and lie on the bed done up in magenta scarves. I will perhaps have my hair carroted as a nice little surprise.'[52] After one reunion, H.D. suggestively conveys her happiness: 'How sweet to see, to smell, to taste Fido again.'[53] The two tease each other constantly, in barely coded language. Bryher looks forward to the day 'he will bite the ankles of his own own Baby Horse, Pretty Horse, pretty baby Horse, Horse'; cautions H.D. to 'be careful of your rump'; and asks for a good olive oil rub on her own rear flanks.[54] From the early 1920s until the end of their lives, they bestowed animal names on their entire circle. Robert was 'Bob-cat', Marianne Moore 'Dactyl', Dorothy Richardson was 'Rat', Helen Doolittle 'Beaver' and so on. 'Zoo', in their letters, might refer to a collection of wild animals – Bryher was obsessed with zoos. Or it might refer to sex.

H.D. and Bryher were creating a queer family, within a queer circle. There was a 'fluidity in sexual practice' between them, each willing to 'play "boy" roles' and to 'turn the "man" in a same-sex relationship'.[55] On gender, Susan McCabe confirms, 'Both sought a nonbinary view of their bodies, history, and the cosmos, and in fact, "gender queer" accurately applies to H.D., who identified as male and female.'[56] What is more, the degree to which the two were what today would be termed 'sex-positive' cannot be understated. Their community included Stein and Toklas; film-maker Marc Allégret (André Gide's 'nephew'); Edith Sitwell's brother Osbert and his long-time partner David Stuart Horner; writers Compton and Faith Mackenzie; Natalie Barney, and those who frequented her Sapphic salon; novelist Katharine Burdekin (Murray Constantine) and her lover Isobel; playwright Thornton Wilder; poet Muriel Rukeyser; closeted psychoanalyst Walter Schmideberg and his wife Melitta (daughter of renowned psychoanalyst Melanie Klein); poet May Sarton; Cornelia Brookfield and her partner Ellen Hart, both writers and translators; writer and editor Robert Herring; Marianne Moore and her mother (a lesbian, who shared her bed with her daughter);[57] Beach, Monnier and Beach's later lover, the photographer Gisèle Freund; sexologist Gavin Arthur and his wife, Charlie, a lesbian; and the novelist Elizabeth Bowen. Even their straight friends lived unconventional sexual lives. H.D. was on friendly terms with both Ezra Pound's wife and his extramarital partner, Olga Rudge. Their friend Nancy Cunard scandalized London with her open interracial relationship with jazz musician Henry Crowder. Havelock Ellis was happily married to a lesbian. Bryher herself was born out of wedlock.

Their circle also included Norman Douglas, whose exploits with young girls and (especially) boys (his 'crocodiles') were open knowledge among his intimates, including H.D. and Bryher, who helped support him for three decades. 'You don't even give me a chance of guessing whether you are male or female,' his mischievous first missive to Bryher read, 'Not that these things matter greatly, nowadays!'[58] With Bryher, who became particularly close to him, he shared details of his sexual escapades, going so far, at one point, as to lament the expensive rates demanded by Italian families for access to their children.[59] From these economically deprived boys, Norman was interested in sex and housekeeping services. To Perdita, however, who remembered him fondly, he was simply 'Uncle Norman', a member of the family who bounced her affectionately on his knee while feeding her small amounts of snuff and wine. It was on a visit to see him, as an adult, that she met for the first and only time, by chance, her father. Cecil Gray was among Norman's entourage.[60]

H.D. and Bryher's relationship was, necessarily if not always easily, an open one. H.D. was bisexual and insisted upon, as she had with Aldington, expressing her sexuality without constraints. She was still seeing Frances Gregg and Brigit Patmore. She had a crush on Brigit's friend Doris Leslie, an actor and popular novelist whose beauty enchanted H.D., and she pursued liaisons with men as well, including the literary critic H. P. Collins and Andrew Gibson, a friend of Gregg's who appears in H.D.'s novella 'Narthex'. Friends and lovers, gossip and intrigue, seducing and being seduced were important to H.D. because they were vital to her creative process. 'Writing and life were not diametric opposites,' she affirmed in *Asphodel*.[61] One fuelled the other.

It is no exaggeration to say that Gregg and Patmore tormented H.D. She was loyal to a fault, but she also found herself weak in the face of their charms. Gregg's letters to H.D. oscillated between venom and sentiment; H.D. opened a discarded novel with the observation that Gregg 'says everything two ways'.[62] Frances called her ugly and cast aspersions on her, even while gushing, 'You were always miles and eons and worlds ahead of me in sheer brain and gifts.'[63] A romantic, Patmore was still scribbling lines to H.D. like these in 1924: 'I find myself writing intense bits to you – about you & what I feel for you,' and 'my heart finds you flawless'.[64] She would go on to write two autobiographical novels about H.D. Both Gregg and Patmore had fallen on hard times. Brigit had left her abusive husband and was working as an usher – unheard of for a middle-class woman in this period – to support herself and her sons. Frances narrowly escaped an attempt by her husband and his friend, the infamous occultist Aleister Crowley, to imprison her in a mental institution.[65] Newly divorced in 1923, she, too, was a single mother, and in 1926 she nearly died of cancer. H.D. sympathized with their plights and provided emotional support to both women, sending them hand-me-down clothing and other 'gifts' to help them get by. She read manuscripts and tried to help them get published. Brigit doted on Perdita, and Brigit's son proclaimed that he planned to marry H.D. when he grew up.[66] H.D. spent time with Frances's children but balked at Frances's scheme to orchestrate a future marriage between Perdita and her son, Oliver.

Despite her fierce commitment to Bryher, H.D. required freedom to pursue other desires. Ellis had, in fact, warned Bryher early on against trying to control H.D.: 'it is absolutely necessary to share her as much as possible,' he advised, 'or she might fly away.'[67] In 1924, H.D. cautioned Bryher,

> always remember that a very wild horse has been trimmed down and kept pretty close in its paddock for some five years. Not that it wanted to kick up its heels and have twenty stallions at it, but after all, it needs a certain amount of free roaming . . . if the gates clang too tight, I shall one day, in spite of myself, simply jump the fence and perhaps never come back.[68]

Bryher agreed, but only to a point. In an endearing bit of verse later that year, she reminds H.D. to mind her feelings:

> REMEMBER FIDO IS NOT STONE.
> HE IS A FAT DELIRIOUS BONE
> LAID AT THE HOOVES OF HORSE ALONE.[69]

Much more prone to jealousy than H.D., Bryher would continue to struggle with H.D.'s other lovers, but she had her own amorous adventures and was open about her crushes on other women. Early on, she and Marianne Moore cultivated a romantic friendship, mostly in letters.[70] While Bryher's initial tendency was always to resist the temptations of cities like Paris and, later, Berlin, she eventually gave herself over to the pleasures of city nightlife. On one trip to Paris, she excitedly shares with H.D. falling in love at first sight with a young 'Polish Jewess' at a lesbian bar where 'scores of beautiful pumas danc[ed] together'.[71] 'Fido takes to the smoke and pumas', Bryher enthused, 'like Perdita to a train!'[72]

All the while, they were raising Perdita, a rambunctious, precocious child. Their Swiss neighbours were never quite sure whose child she was.[73] 'I had two mothers,' Perdita explained: 'My real mother, H.D., who lived on an exceedingly rarefied plane. And her surrogate, Bryher, who took care of reality.'[74] H.D. was

H.D. and Perdita,
1920s.

there for emotional comfort and affection. Bryher loved to get
down on the floor with her and play with her toys. Perdita read
with H.D., and planned adventures with Bryher. H.D. indulged
her. Bryher disciplined her. Her mothers possessed quite different
temperaments: as Perdita once quipped to H.D., 'Fido cuts the
knots, but you untangle them.'[75] They both loved her, however. 'In
their different ways, both mothers gave me a lot of affection. I felt
cherished,' she recalled.[76]

    H.D. adhered to a strict, tightly regimented writing schedule.
She needed solitude, unlike Bryher, who could focus easily in the

midst of chaos.[77] While the household conspired to rigorously guard H.D.'s writing time, Perdita could always curl up in her mother's lap while she was reading.[78] In Switzerland, H.D. and her daughter took long late morning strolls down to the stunningly picturesque port of Territet, feeding crumbs to birds on Lake Geneva.[79] They laughed together. In London in the early to mid-1920s H.D. was her sole caregiver; Perdita's days were divided between quiet play in the morning while H.D. wrote, and afternoons of makeshift picnics and walks in Kensington Gardens.[80] In later years, Perdita recounted a happy childhood, her only complaint the instability created by the women's restlessness. Even so – once deemed old enough to accompany them – she relished trips to the United States, France, Germany, Italy, Greece and South Africa. Like Bryher, a young Perdita had wanderlust. Desperately wanting to become a sailor and go to sea, she once packed her bags and ran away from home, Liberia her intended destination.[81]

Eventually, in the spring of 1928, amidst fears of legal reprisal from Richard Aldington, Bryher would formally adopt Perdita. Though she had initially been reticent about having a child, Bryher quickly came to embrace H.D.'s daughter, taking charge of her education, eager to correct the mistakes of her own Victorian schooling. H.D. approved of home-schooling her daughter; in an autobiographical novel, H.D.'s narrator decries 'the process of civilizing, of schooling' as 'devitalizing'.[82] (Their instincts were correct: Perdita's brief stint in an English boarding school failed miserably.) With lessons by Bryher, H.D. and a string of governesses and tutors, Perdita knew four languages by the age of five. She already had 'a typewriter and a room of [her] own', and was working away at a surprisingly lengthy autobiography – having inherited from both mothers a penchant for fictionalizing her life – and writing adventure stories not unlike those that entertained Bryher as a child.[83]

Indeed, until she went through adolescence, Perdita was
very much like Bryher, a kinship signified by a canine familial
nickname, 'Pup': 'The hopeless blunder of being a girl was my
greatest bone of contention with life,' Perdita complained, in
language that resonates with Bryher's account of her own youth.
'It made the future so dull . . . My only salvation lay in somehow
switching my sex . . . I was a boy at heart, and had gone astray.' 'My
reading had to be smeared with blood', she continued, 'and roaring
with wild animals.'[84] She cut out Christians from scrap paper and
tossed them to her stuffed lions.[85]

Their animated, itinerant existence inspired H.D., who wrote
a great deal of verse and prose in the 1920s. In her essays on Greek
poets, she had honoured Meleager as of 'the aube, pre-dawn,
white-violet, symbolical of that very spirit of beauty and toleration
and exquisite humility that condoned and exonerated those who
had "loved much".'[86] Named for the love of Meleager's life, her
second volume of poetry of the 1920s was *Heliodora*, published by
Jonathan Cape in 1924. *Heliodora* interweaves her own Greek verse
translations and those of Plato, Nossis, Meleager and Sappho, and
several of the volume's poems contemplate the processes of writing
and translation, imagining collaborations between poets – 'a
compositional strategy', Steven Yao has demonstrated, 'by which she
assimilates the masculine tradition of writing about women with
her own project of writing as a woman.'[87] *Heliodora* also includes
more verse from the perspective of female Greek mythological
figures, as well as one of her best-known poems, 'Helen', a critique of
the blazon. The face, the hands, the mouth, the knees, the feet of the
infamously beautiful Helen of Troy are not the object of desire but
of revulsion: 'All Greece hates/ the still eyes in the white face . . . All
Greece reviles/ the wan face when she smiles.' Greece can only love
her 'if she were laid,/ white ash amid funereal cypresses'.[88]

In 1925, H.D.'s reputation as an Imagist poet was solidified
with the Boni & Liveright publication of *Collected Poems of H.D.*

However, this post-First World War period is noteworthy, too, for her turn to prose. In the 1920s, having reached some maturity, H.D. was in a period of reflection. *Paint It Today* was the first of four autobiographical novels (including *Asphodel*, HER*mione* and *Bid Me to Live*) fictionalizing the tumultuous years between H.D.'s twin courtships with Gregg and Pound in Pennsylvania, and Bryher's entrance into her life a decade later. Here we see H.D.'s life literally becoming her art. She initially intended to publish *Paint It Today*, but her prose efforts were met with resistance from publishers who expected her to remain purely 'H.D.', the poet who produced exquisite 'crystalline' Imagist poems. H.D. found this not just irritating but disheartening. To chronicler of Imagism Glenn Hughes, she defended her prose:

> the ones who deigned to notice my prose seemed rather shocked by it . . . But I have to go on my own way. A critic in London, who had professed great admiration for my verse, said when he saw my first prose MSS, 'but, H.D. you must not publish this . . . you have your NICHE in London'. One of the unforgivable literary crimes is, I believe, stepping out of one's niche.[89]

Ultimately undeterred, she continued writing short and long fiction for the rest of her life. 'I can't be held up by what the critics think H.D. ought to be like,' she wrote to a friend.[90] Fiction that was rejected was printed privately or circulated in manuscript form among those in her circle.

Paint It Today, probably written around 1920, is the most lyrical of the four books. It focuses almost entirely on her relationships with Frances Gregg and Bryher, barely mentioning her marriage or her writing. It is in this first foray into fiction that she introduces a self-reflexive mode of autobiography that will prove to be the hallmark of her oeuvre. Anticipating contemporary theorizing of life writing, H.D. portrays not a unitary self – autonomous, agentive, unified and unitary – but a fragmented self, the self as both subject and object of narration. H.D. is not the book's author ('Helga Dart' appears on the title page), nor is she the narrator (the 'I' of the book, whom others call Miss Defreddie) or the main character (Midget). Yet all are versions of Hilda Doolittle, at once distinctive and indistinguishable. Guarding against the tendency to conflate the *I*s, she nonetheless acknowledges the appeal of doing so: 'I will not let *I* creep into this story,' the narrator tells us. 'I will not let *I* go on banging the tinkling cymbal of its own emotion. You and I are out of this story, are observing.'[91]

H.D. employs the autobiographical mode with a frequency unmatched among high modernists. Though her prose style shifts markedly after the 1930s, her understanding of the complexities of the autobiographical *I* does not. Her prose insists adamantly on both the fictionality and truth of autobiography. In a reflective essay written in 1949–50, she records her responses to rereading her earlier work, noting the long list of characters based on herself even while distancing herself from them. She is, she writes, all of these figures, and at the same time, 'We are not one or any of those whose lovely names startle and enchant me, as I read them now as if for the first time, in my own prose and poetry.'[92]

Asphodel was written close on the heels of *Paint It Today* and covers roughly the same time period, bookending the text with the end of her first affair with Gregg and the beginning of her relationship with Bryher, but devoting the centre of it to her marriage and stillbirth. Abandoning the prose-poem rhythms of her first novel, she adopts a stream-of-consciousness technique for her second. Elliptical, elusive, raw, the flow of the narrator's thoughts surges across the traumatic span of the war years. Dedicated to Gregg, *HERmione* was penned in the late 1920s and offers a kind of prequel to *Asphodel*, setting the scene in Pennsylvania – before her exodus to Europe – when a young Hilda became a writer and fell in love with Gregg and Pound.

As in *Asphodel*, H.D. is Hermione, or Her, H.D.'s wordplay here emphasizing again the self as object of narration.

Over a decade later, her final account of the early years was written, *Bid Me to Live* (originally titled *Madrigal*). The only one of the four published during her lifetime, it erases any trace of lesbian desire, and the form it takes is more conventional than its predecessors. With her legacy firmly in mind, this version of the dissolution of her marriage was entwined with the story of her brief friendship with D. H. Lawrence. The novel, however, becomes more about the narrator's assertion of her worth as a woman writer than about Lawrence himself.

A manifesto, two books of verse, a collected edition of her poetry, three autobiographical novels – all produced between 1919 and 1926. But H.D. wrote still more in this era, including over a dozen reviews of books on antiquity and art for H. P. Collins's *Adelphi*; several short stories and abandoned novels; a verse drama, *Hippolytus Temporizes*; and three historical novels. The first of these historical novels was inspired in part by a memorable trip to Egypt. For Bryher, Egypt was a favoured site from her childhood that she wished to share with H.D.: for H.D., Egypt was the source of Greek religion and culture. H.D.'s mother Helen Doolittle, now widowed, was just eager to see the world.

In the winter of 1923, on the heels of a 1922 trip to Greece and Constantinople, Bryher, H.D. and Helen journeyed to Egypt and cruised the Nile, exploring temples, islands and the ruins of Cairo and Luxor, the Pyramids of Giza, the Valley of the Kings and the Valley of the Queens. They toured museums, shopped at bazaars and bookstores and saw Karnak by moonlight. Their trip coincided with the celebrated opening of the burial chamber of King Tutankhamun, which had been discovered two months earlier. Helen went on to Florence, while H.D. and Bryher stayed in Capri for six weeks, seeing friends Nancy Cunard and Norman Douglas there. Helen and Perdita joined them in Capri for Perdita's fourth birthday.

H.D. in Egypt, 1923.

H.D. had familiarized herself with the vast Egyptology collection at the British Museum, but this trip was undoubtedly foundational for her. Composed after her return from Egypt, *Palimpsest* came out with Contact Press in 1926 and was widely reviewed. The three discrete stories about women writers and scholars are meant to be read, as its title indicates, as a palimpsest, their traces bleeding into one another. A novel in three parts – or 'three long-short stories'[93] – the first, 'Hipparchia', retells the story of her separation from Aldington and liaison with Gray, placing the characters in ancient Rome, after the conquering of Greece in the Battle of Corinth in 146 BCE. A displaced Greek, Hipparchia is a poet dedicated to keeping the Greek spirit alive and a consort to an unfaithful Roman soldier. The setting makes the story as much about the brutality of imperialism as it is about infidelity, and she recycles the tale yet again in the second story of *Palimpsest*, 'Murex', but with a different aim. In 'Murex', the focus shifts quickly from infidelity to the art that emerges out of trauma. In the depths of despair, her protagonist, Raymonde, writes herself out of her despondency. The final part, 'Secret Name: Excavator's Egypt', features Helen Fairwood, assistant to a prominent Egyptologist, who tours the ruins and temples of Luxor and has a spiritual experience one moonlit night in the Valley of the Kings.

While these stories go over some of the same ground as her other novels of the period, the genre of historical fiction also affords H.D. the opportunity to analyse the politics of imperialism and gender, and to explore ways women writers can, and can't, intervene. 'Nothing in the epiphanies of the three women changes the external structures of society that initiated their interior conflicts,' Susan Stanford Friedman comments; 'the politics of empire and bedroom are unchanged.'[94] In this sense, the book serves as a powerful commentary on the ways in which the personal is always political. Historically, the English have been invested in a portrait of their civilization as indebted to the ancient Romans, who had landed on their shores in 43 CE. The London Museum still begins its tour with a pictorial exhibit that shows primitive ape-like British figures morphing into erect, Roman *Homo sapiens*. H.D.'s prose offers a counter-narrative: her literary history traces the seeds of English literature to ancient Greece, and not to Rome. The writer's role is to read the palimpsest, to unveil the traces of Greek art and culture in those of Rome. Her work on Egypt decades later will perform a similar function by exposing civilizations – Egyptian, Babylonian, Assyrian – that preceded that of her beloved Greece.

Around the same time, H.D. was also writing *Pilate's Wife*, a historical novel set during the time of the crucifixion of Jesus – a narrative thread that, upon reading D. H. Lawrence's *The Man Who Died*, she believed had been stolen from her. The novel's main character is the fictionalized wife of Pontius Pilate, whom H.D. dubs Veronica, who is plagued by two questions, one anchored in a crisis of religion and the other in a crisis of identity. A fortune-teller (not a little reminiscent of Frances Gregg) leads her to 'a sort of poet, a young Jew', and Veronica conspires to save Jesus' life and to find sanctuary for him outside of Jerusalem.[95] H.D. was dismayed when Ferris Greenslet of Houghton Mifflin rejected the novel for publication, claiming that it lacked 'the intensity of emotion that made [*Palimpsest*] memorable'.[96] It was not published during her lifetime.

The third historical novel of this period, *Hedylus*, was drafted around the same time as the others; it was published by Basil Blackwell and Houghton Mifflin in 1928. As with *Paint It Today*, it bears an intensely lyrical style, which Edith Sitwell, to H.D.'s delight, termed 'hallucinated'.[97] The titular protagonist is a young poet who fortuitously encounters his long-lost father at the very moment in his life when he is trying to decide his future. As in 'Hipparchia', Hedylus and his beautiful but ageing mother Hedyle – a 'stylized exiled Athenian hetaera'[98] – are deracinated Greeks. In this novel, they quarrel over Hedylus' love for the boyish Irene, and

H.D., late 1920s.

in this young man, 'who had always been striving self with self',
there are thus traces of H.D., Perdita and Bryher.[99]

Looking back, H.D. would read *Hedylus* alongside her
translation of Euripides' *Hippolytus Temporizes* as 'portrait[s] or
projection[s] of the intellectualized, crystalline youth'.[100] H.D.'s
verse-drama translation was not written quickly: it was begun in
1920 at Corfu and completed in London in 1926, appearing in 1927
with Houghton Mifflin Press. Euripides' dark drama is based on
the ancient Greek myth of Theseus' son, Hippolytus, begotten from
the rape of the Amazon Hippolyta. Aphrodite seeks vengeance on
the chaste Hippolytus for his preference for Artemis by inducing
his stepmother, Phaedra, to fall in love with him. When Phaedra
kills herself, Theseus erroneously blames his son, casting him out
of the kingdom. Hippolytus is mortally wounded in an accident,
and he and his father – chastened by Artemis – are reconciled
before he dies. More an adaptation than translation, H.D.'s far
bleaker version cuts Theseus' presence and Aphrodite's lines,

shifting the focus to Phaedra's seduction of Hippolytus (successful in her version), his melancholic attachment to his mother, and his tortured pursuit of Artemis. She concludes the play with a lengthy debate between Artemis and Helios over sexual mores and the fate of the mangled body of a dying Hippolytus. The madness of unrequited love and lust rests at the centre of her play.

H.D. does not stop writing poetry or fiction at the end of 1926, but she does begin to work in another medium, one that promised 'new vision' and 'fresh/ hope'.[101] H.D.'s and Bryher's film-making career begins when H.D. meets and falls in love with a young, queer Scottish artist and writer, Kenneth Macpherson.

5

'the perfect bi-', 1927–39

Bryher's impulsive marriage to Robert McAlmon had been doomed to fail. Perdita reflected about those years, 'He came and went. The mothers complained when he went. When he came, they were a quarrelsome trio. Voices were raised, tables pounded, doors slammed.'[1] McAlmon's memoir, *Being Geniuses Together*, was far less kind, bitterly representing himself and H.D. as victims of Bryher's emotional manipulation. The acrimonious comments of an ex-husband aside, it is clear that the marriage could not continue. Robert's life was one long party. He had imagined their arrangement would require very little time spent in London with her parents. Bryher had imagined a more discreet partner, a more convincing 'beard'.

Even so, Bryher feared the sensational publicity around a divorce. In the 1920s, the Ku Klux Klan collected and publicized information about Americans divorcing abroad. Her concern was not misplaced. The press was not kind. William Bird, an erstwhile friend, published a scathing tidbit of gossip about them that was syndicated widely in the United States and Britain, baldly revealing that the marriage had been merely a ploy by Bryher to gain independence from her parents.[2] Hemingway reputedly referred to McAlmon as 'McAlimony'.

The marriage with Robert had provided H.D. and Bryher necessary cover. Kenneth Macpherson's entrance into their lives, then, was fortuitous. Macpherson was a writer, artist, film-maker and amateur designer descended from a long line of artists, his formal training in the commercial arts. He met Frances Gregg when they became neighbours; according to her son, Oliver, she fell in love with him before introducing him to H.D., thus creating another love triangle between the two women and a man.[3] Macpherson, however, was not tempted by Frances, as Ezra Pound had been. Macpherson and H.D. were passionately smitten with each other. In an autobiographical novella composed a few years later, she implied that their sexual relationship was so fulfilling because they resisted commitment to gender assignment.[4] They were perfectly matched.

Bryher and Robert had fought constantly. Kenneth and Bryher, however, became fast friends – taking long walks together in Chillon woods, furiously planning artistic projects together. Despite being fifteen years younger than H.D., Kenneth, at least in the early years, blended more harmoniously with the family than Robert had. Even eight-year-old Perdita wanted to run away with him, 'to some desert island where we could be together and eat coconuts and swim, and talk forever without being disturbed'.[5] So in June of 1927 Bryher divorced McAlmon, and in September she wed Macpherson in a lavender marriage that had the additional benefit of re-establishing her British citizenship, lost when she had married an American. With Perdita and a revolving cadre of cats, dogs and monkeys, the threesome settled in Switzerland.

Mixing male, female and neutral pronouns in letters to H.D. and Bryher, Macpherson falls seamlessly into their coded animal language. Sly references to rumps and spanking abound. H.D. is transformed from 'Horse' to 'Kat' (or 'Lynx') in the *ménage*'s effusive correspondence of the period, while Kenneth ('Rover' or 'Big Dog') and Bryher ('Fido' or 'Small Dog') adopt canine nicknames. Perdita, apparently less canine as she approached adolescence, is less 'Pup' than 'Puss', as she becomes aligned with H.D. 'Still Dog and DOG (that's me) do miss its kikken,' Kenneth writes to H.D., 'and long to

Perdita with pet monkey.

rub their noses in the furry ruffle round its neck, and hope it won't scratch too hard.'[6] 'It is Dog's own kikken, and do do do do do take care of every one of its paws and lives, and write to its dog all its kat ideas of kat news,' he ends another letter.[7] Bryher concludes a letter to Kenneth that she 'trust[s] that he has sun & warmth for the behind of his tail'.[8] Comedic sketches of Rover, and often Fido and Lynx, fill the margins of Kenneth's letters to both, and together they constructed a scrapbook of collages documenting their lives. The threesome filled the house with the sounds of typewriters, monkey screeches, high-flown talk of aesthetics and Kenneth's gramophone. And laughter. H.D.'s carefully curated public persona concealed a wicked sense of humour and 'a spontaneous wit which seized the absurdities of life and everyone's foibles, including her own'.[9]

Macpherson introduced H.D. and Bryher to film-making. H.D. had long been a movie fan, so it was no surprise perhaps that she quickly became entranced. Describing herself as 'a cat playing with webs and webs of silver', H.D. reported to the *Little Review* that she was spending hours alone with their film projector.[10] Two oracular poems entitled 'Projector' worship the medium, in which

> light reasserts
> his power
> reclaims the lost;
> in a blaze of splendour.[11]

A fundamentally democratic medium that empowers the disempowered, film, for H.D., imagines we can 'live lives that might have been,/ live lives that ever are'.[12] It is a medium both therapeutic and inspiring, for it brings us

> light,
> light that sears and breaks
> us
> from old doubts
> and fears.[13]

Never having been a moviegoer, Bryher had to be coaxed, but upon seeing German film-maker G. W. Pabst's *Joyless Street* – a film H.D. called 'the most astonishingly consistently lovely film I have ever seen'[14] – she quickly came around. Within months of meeting Macpherson, Bryher had founded POOL Books and POOL

Films. The POOL Group established a short-lived but flourishing avant-garde film community in Territet; film luminaries like Pabst and the Soviet director Sergei Eisenstein were frequent visitors. Macpherson's aesthetic, at once impressionistic and surrealist, owed a great deal to Eisenstein's use of camera angles and montage, and he admired, too, Pabst's psychological realism. Macpherson and Bryher (and occasionally H.D.) travelled regularly to Berlin – dubbed the birthplace of experimental film by Bryher – submerging themselves in its gay subcultures and haunting its avant-garde theatres, viewing as many as five to six films per week when they were in the German capital.[15] Letters home recounted lengthy descriptions of films seen, parties attended and people encountered.

POOL Books published very little – eight books in total, and none by H.D. – but POOL Films would become far more significant historically. In a sense, these were still early days for film, and POOL launched the first serious film journal, *Close Up*, in July of 1927. 'It represented', according to contemporary film scholars James Donald, Anne Friedberg and Laura Marcus, 'a major attempt by a group of literary intellectuals to assess, at a crucial moment of transition, the aesthetic possibilities opened up by cinema within, despite and against its commercial contexts'.[16] Its goal, in Friedberg's words, was to promote 'a cinema that mirrored the aesthetics and production of their own written discourse: discourse about the object, artfully designed, psychologically astute'.[17] Seeming often to be at war with itself – at times anti-Hollywood, at others critical of the avant-garde – it brought an idiosyncratic but capacious vision of film into view.

Close Up's success – it sold out its first print run of five hundred copies and ran over six years – astounded Bryher, who had put up a mere £60 because she expected it, at best, to fare about as well as other small-circulation literary magazines.[18] Advocating silent film as transcending national boundaries, the journal had an international reach, in terms of both its readership and its diverse contributors, which included directors, actors, artists, photographers, journalists, historians, playwrights, set designers, activists, cinematographers, documentarians, psychoanalysts and film critics, as well as modernist women writers Gertrude Stein, Marianne Moore and Dorothy Richardson. It printed film criticism and theory by Japanese, German, Soviet, Czech, Swiss, French, British and American writers, and treated not just European and American (including African American) film but the cinema of Russia, Japan, India and South America.

In the first two years of the journal's publication, H.D. contributed two poems and eleven articles, including a tribute to Pabst, a three-part series on 'The Cinema and the Classics', an essay on Russian and English cinema, a commentary on the cinematic elements of Noël Coward's play *Sirocco*, and reviews of films by Austrian, American, Russian and Danish directors. In essays that evidence her expert knowledge of cinematic technique, a recurring focus is the spectator's visceral or somatic response to formal elements of film. As her poetry about film suggests, she enjoyed immersion in a cinematic landscape, appreciating the sense of being a participant in another world. But only to a point. She was troubled by Hollywood excess, wondering why directors overstuff a scene when a singular image will do. She also disliked manipulation, such as that effected by Carl Dreyer's claustrophobic set, slow pace and reliance on extreme close-ups in *La Passion de Jeanne d'Arc*. 'Do I have to be cut into slices by this inevitable pan-movement of the camera, these suave lines to left, up, to the right, back, all rhythmical with the remorseless rhythm of a scimitar?', H.D. demands to know.[19] Unnerved, she returns to the film in a later essay: 'It positively bullied me as no film has yet done . . . I was forced to pity, pity, pity. My affections and credulity were hammered. I was kicked. I was throttled. I was laid upon a torture rack.'[20]

H.D.'s contributions to *Close Up* broadly condemn the Hollywood and English film traditions in favour of contemporary German and Russian cinema. 'The great new Russian idea is not to make star personalities,' she remarks pointedly, 'but to let personalities make stars.'[21] Taking Greta Garbo as an example – Bryher, Macpherson and H.D. were positively obsessed with her – H.D. criticizes Hollywood for *The Torrent*, in which Garbo appears as 'deflowered, deracinated, devitalized', alleging that Americans can only conceive of a beautiful woman as 'a vamp, an evil woman', swathing her in gaudy makeup and outlandish costumes.[22] Garbo in *Joyless Street*, by contrast, was a 'grave, sweet creature before America claimed her'.[23] She excoriates Hollywood for its anti-feminism: '*Must* Beauty always dress itself in scarlet, drag sumptuous velours about apparently naked limbs?'[24] Indeed, women's roles were another common thread in these essays, and on this topic, she wrote, Pabst is to be applauded. Surveying rich performances by Garbo and Brigitte Helm, H.D. asserts that 'Pabst brings out the vital and vivid forces in women,' and, 'All the women of Herr Pabst's creation . . . have "another side" to them.'[25]

The group wasn't just writing about film. They were making film. Macpherson saw in H.D. a movie star, and though a novice she was surprisingly skilled and magnetic on-screen. Macpherson reported Pabst's assessment of H.D. on film: 'how STRONG is H.D., it is amazing, how strong, what power, how consistent . . . [she] showed up the utter futility of the Hollywood tradition and that beauty was something quite different.'[26] A boyish, closely shorn H.D. made her film debut in Macpherson's *Wing Beat*, a plotless, surrealist attempt 'to translate Imagism into film'.[27] The plot of their next movie, *Foothills*, followed 'a dame from the city (H.[D.]) [who] comes to the country village for rest . . . all the complications of village life and gossip and a sort of idealistic encounter with the young intelligent lout who is K[enneth] in Vaudois farm clothes'.[28] Only fragments of these efforts survive, but two of their films

H.D. film still, late 1920s.

are extant. The first of these was in 1929, a short, *Monkey's Moon*, starring douroucouli monkeys who escape their captors to revel in an outdoor escapade before being captured and returned to their cages.

Their most significant endeavour, however, was *Borderline*, a film about racial violence and interracial desire – a film that Pabst called 'the only real avant-garde film'.[29] Its method is experimental, relying heavily on montage and abstraction with a highly tuned sense of the visual. H.D.'s extended essay promoting the film proclaims that 'Macpherson has achieved a sort of dynamic picture writing,' though in fact it was she and Bryher who had done the post-production editing.[30] H.D. was interested in learning both ends of the camera lens. 'At the moment,' she told the *Little Review*,

I want to go on in this medium . . . experimenting with faces and shadows and corners . . . I should like more than anything to have some sort of . . . little car that I could work myself and go off and on, on my own, more or less to Italy and wander in and about Italian and Swiss hills making light do what I want . . . I can do a little work on the small cameras and some of it will be incorporated in the big film that we are busy on.[31]

That 'big film', *Borderline*, featured African American singer and actor Paul Robeson, who had already begun to attain global renown. Set in a provincial Swiss town, the silent film centres around an interracial affair between a white man and a Black woman, played by Robeson's wife, Eslanda. H.D. stars in the role of a virulently racist scorned wife, Robeson the wronged husband. The villagers' ire is directed solely at the Black couple, as the film exposes the culpability of the white characters. When Robeson's character is cast out after violence erupts, flickering images of a lynching make clear the position of the film-makers.

H.D., to be clear, was no activist, but she was disturbed by racial violence and injustice in the States. Both Bryher and Macpherson spent a significant amount of time in Harlem in this period, and Bryher contributed financial support for Harlem Renaissance artists. Regarding H.D.'s short story 'Two Americans', which fictionalizes an evening spent with the Robesons, H.D. wrote to Bryher that she found much literature about Black Americans so 'Horrible' that she felt she must offer a corrective: 'Time something was done'.[32] Eslanda's diary recounts that though the Robesons found Macpherson and H.D. painfully 'naive' about race, 'We never once felt we were colored with them.'[33] It is also true that both Kenneth and H.D. were erotically drawn to Paul; Macpherson would later become jealous when reading H.D.'s poem 'Red Roses for Bronze', a sensual account of sculpting a bronze statue of a man probably inspired by Robeson.

Unlike Macpherson's other efforts, *Borderline* was screened widely in art-house theatres across Europe – in the UK, Germany, Belgium, Spain, Holland and Denmark – though probably not in

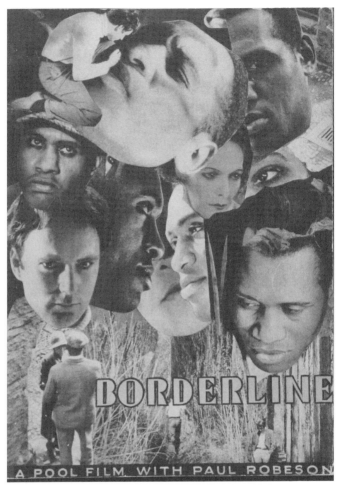

Borderline poster, 1930.

the United States due to its portrayal of an interracial couple. It was also more widely reviewed than POOL's other films. Its detractors deplored its experimental approach to film-making, but glowing reviews noted its leftist themes and its technique.[34]

H.D.'s poetry of the period takes a decided turn toward performance. In the late 1920s and early 1930s she produces a number of translations of ancient Greek drama by the playwright she most admired, Euripides, including excerpts of *The Bacchae* and *Hecuba* in *Red Roses for Bronze* (1930), parts of *Electra* and *Orestes* in her unpublished volume *The Dead Priestess Speaks,* and the entirety of *Hippolytus Temporizes* and *Ion.* Noting H.D.'s lifelong fascination with this ancient Greek playwright, Eileen Gregory points out: 'No modernist poet shows a greater literary exchange with an ancient writer.' Gregory contends that H.D. was attracted to his scepticism about war and patriotism, to his lyricism and use of the choral voice and to his mysticism.[35] She was drawn, too, to his female characters and the psychological depth of his depictions of family dynamics.

Much of her late 1920s and early 1930s verse is marked by truncated staccato lines, as she strives to achieve some semblance of ancient Greek rhythm in modern-day English. Sound is dominated by repetition and resonance, stressed syllables crowd into brief lines, and the effect is incantatory, as if she is summoning the gods. In *Ion,* the brevity and heavily stressed cadences induce a sombre and reverential tone. When Queen Kreousa appears onstage, she is like a statue, 'inhuman', god-like. Ion's response – in lines of mostly two to four syllables – reveals his veneration, as if his awed tone has the power to call her forth into being:

O, goddess,
what rain
mars that marble,
your face?
eyes shut
in a mask[36]

Emphasizing polyvocality and community, choral speeches are frequent selections from these texts, a choice that yields a fluid

H.D. in *Borderline*, 1930.

dynamic of inquiry, consensus and dissent. To maintain this
tone, she breaks with the conventional long speeches of Euripides'
original text. By interweaving alternating one-line bits of speeches
between two characters, she achieves the effect of a swift exchange
in which one character's lines inevitably bleed into the other's,
evoking a communal sense of being. In one scene, Kreousa, a
mother seeking her lost son, meets Ion, a son seeking his lost
mother. Neither is aware that they are searching for one another,
though they speak as one in lines that mirror:

Kreousa		– but your mother?
Ion	I am, maybe –	
Kreousa		– no; what fine stuff –
Ion	– robe of a priest –	
Kreousa		– but your parents?
Ion	I have no clue –	
Kreousa		– ah, the same hurt –

Ion	– what hurt – tell me –
Kreousa	– I have come here –
Ion	– you have come here?[37]

In a play dominated by short, heavily stressed lines delivered slowly and ceremonially, the accelerated pace of these alternating lines is striking enough to shift the tenor of the play. It is a novel technique that underscores the intense dramatic irony of the moment, even as it renders identity unstable.

H.D.'s fiction at this time – primarily short stories and novellas – likewise reflects her work in film. As Perdita would recall in a preface to one of these novellas, 'My family was into filmmaking at that time, and it shows. H.D. has reversed the process – and also carried it a stage further – pretending the book is really a film. Her technique is cinematic, a restless dizzying montage.'[38] They are among the most experimental of her prose writings as well. 'Narthex' – based on a trip to Venice – is a study in stream of consciousness that critiques its own method. She followed it with 'The Usual Star', which relies on repetition to achieve an almost cubist effect. *Nights* tends towards surrealism. Of the many short stories and novellas of the period, *Kora and Ka* is perhaps the most abstract. It features a male protagonist suffering from survivor's guilt after a war that took two of his brothers, and readers are held captive within his madness. His rage takes the form of sadism against his lover, as H.D. interrogates the gender dynamics of the aftermath of war. H.D. is interested in pain: how and why humans seek it out, how tenuous the line between pleasure and pain can be, and how pain can work to destabilize identity. Much of this work explores darkness, but it is not nihilistic. There are comic moments in 'The Usual Star' and *Nights*.

Response to these narrative experiments was mixed. H.D. reported to the writer Conrad Aiken that Havelock Ellis adjudged this work 'remarkable', and Aiken himself offered a frank assessment – not entirely complimentary – that pleased her because he praised her innovative form: 'what you are doing with <u>form</u> interests me profoundly – what a lot of things lie ahead in that path! I hope you're going to do them.'[39] She treasured the carefully worded review of Marianne Moore, who seemed almost in fear for H.D.'s sanity. Nonetheless, Moore assured her, 'you help one to feel that the battering we endure need not be the last word.'[40] H.D. confided to her friend George Plank,

> The writing, I have found, seems to be for men . . . I don't know if the women resent my taking all that trouble with young men, with men – or whether it doesn't just ring a bell. This is a great surprise to me – in fact, I have almost lost one or two very old friends, but women. The men, who were charming, but did not seem over-interested in my work, blazed up to it and were so beautiful and generous.[41]

While H.D. continued to migrate back and forth between London and Switzerland, Kenneth and Bryher, and Bryher and Perdita, were travelling the world. There were trips to such far-flung places as Iceland and the West Indies, and Perdita cruised the Dalmatian coast with H.D., before a memorable voyage to South Africa. Perdita, who had longed to go to sea from an early age, charmed one courageous captain, who taught her to steer the ship. Switzerland was Bryher's adopted home, however, and she and Kenneth decided to build a modern house in Vaud. Kenneth filmed the construction of this Bauhaus-inspired mansion. The family and their growing collection of pets moved in on 1 September 1931.

They also maintained flats in Kensington during this period, H.D. and Perdita on Sloane Street, Bryher and Macpherson less than half a mile away, near Albert Gate on Hyde Park, between H.D. and Bryher's parents, whose South Audley Street mansion was east of the park. Though there was less subterfuge required at this

Robert Herring, Kenneth Macpherson and Bryher in Iceland, 1929.

point to appease the Ellermans, and Hannah had become a doting grandmother to Perdita, tension between H.D. and Bryher's mother would persist until Hannah's death. H.D. and Perdita continued to spend Christmas – an important holiday to H.D. – away from Bryher.

H.D.'s short story 'The Usual Star', written in 1928, depicts that tension humorously. It also offers us a sense of what a typical day may have been like for H.D., who spent her time in Switzerland writing diligently but afforded herself more time for socializing in London. The picaresque story follows its protagonist, Raymonde Ransome, as she takes her morning walk with her lover Daniel (Kenneth), chatting about film and aesthetics. She then visits her lover Gareth (Bryher), who is hard at work on Arabic studies at her parents' posh estate, where the two spar over Raymonde's reluctance to accept a dinner invitation from Lady Meyer (Hannah Ellerman). On Raymonde's walk home, she endures a farcical chance encounter with Lady Meyer – a 'great eye-y octopus creature', or 'a sort of mackerel on dry land' with 'gaping jaws',[42] whose confidence in her authority, and whose hearing loss, elicit shouted confidences from an unnerved Raymonde. Even more determined to escape dinner at the Meyers, Raymonde quickly makes alternative evening plans with her friend Ermy, a beautiful but wildly histrionic actor-turned-romance-novelist based on Doris Leslie, with whom H.D. was then engaged in a flirtation. She ends up bailing on Ermy when she finds Katherine (Frances Gregg) lurking in the hallway outside her flat. Katherine hurls beastly criticism at Raymonde's writing but is nonetheless welcomed in for an impromptu supper.

H.D. was probably unaware that by the 1930s she had developed a small cult following in the United States, where small-town reading groups – in, for instance, Bakersfield, California; Bluefield, West Virginia; and Greeley, Colorado – were devouring her verse. A review of *Red Roses for Bronze* in the *Dubuque Telegraph Herald and Times* was glowing.[43] But she felt unsettled about her work in this period. To be sure, she was not unproductive in the late 1920s and early 1930s – she wrote poetry, a book-length translation of Euripides' *Hippolytus Temporizes*, film reviews, a children's book with a heroine inspired by Perdita and several short stories and novellas. But she and Bryher were both concerned that she was not keeping up the pace of the previous decade. She struggled to find a sense of purpose: 'I, like most of the people I knew, in England, America, and on the Continent of Europe, was drifting.'[44]

These were not easy years for H.D. Helen Doolittle died in March of 1927. H.D. had an abortion in Berlin in 1928. Her relationship to Kenneth had always been an open one for both, but by the early 1930s Kenneth was increasingly drawn to men. She did not mind these dalliances, but on summer trips to Monte Carlo, she was beginning to feel neglected. The threesome, moreover, were no longer living in harmony. Perdita remembers that 'Everything revolved around H.D. Kenneth and Bryher deferred to her mercurial temperament, worried about her well-being. Little jealousies crept in as they vied for her attention.'[45] H.D. cultivated new lovers in the 1930s. There was another film-maker, Dan Birt. There was Stephen Guest. And there was a young activist, astrologer and budding novelist, Silvia Dobson, whose eyes reminded her of Frances Gregg's. H.D. promptly tired of them. Her squabbles with 'psychic klepto-maniac' Frances escalated.[46] She felt uncomfortable in her own skin. She sensed, too, a terrifying shift in Continental politics that resurrected the traumas of the First World War. In April of 1931, with Bryher's urging, H.D. entered psychoanalysis.

While H.D. had entertained a passing interest in psychoanalysis – having been introduced by Gregg to Freud's writings in the original German in 1911[47] – Bryher was a lifelong follower of the movement, an unwavering believer in its efficacy and a loyal patron. She very nearly, in fact, completed the training to be an analyst herself. Once she had deposited H.D. with an analyst, she bullied an extremely reluctant Macpherson into following suit. Disturbed that her first psychoanalyst, Mary Chadwick (Dan Birt's aunt), did not abide by a rigorous boundary between doctor and patient, H.D. stopped treatment abruptly, and Bryher cajoled her into seeing her own analyst, Hanns Sachs, a close friend of Sigmund Freud and Chadwick's former teacher. When Bryher and Sachs concurred that H.D. must see Freud himself, Freud readily agreed to the arrangement. H.D. relocated to the Hotel Regina in Vienna and eagerly commenced her first round of sessions with Freud, from March to June of 1933.

There was conflict early on. She cried through the first session. She resisted – while he insisted on – the couch. She was horrified by his disdain for felines, demonstrated gleefully in a brutal story of his chow breaking the neck of a cat.[48] He raged at her when she admitted that Freud was a maternal, rather than paternal or romantic, transferential figure for her, beating his fist on the couch: 'The trouble is – I am an old man,' he cried, *you do not think it worth your while to love me*.'[49] He forbade notetaking and reflection between sessions, a rule that ran deeply counter to H.D.'s nature (and sometimes her practice). As he guided her through the plethora of ancient statuary, artefacts and ephemera that filled his room, she did not appreciate his penis envy joke that Niké, goddess of victory, had 'lost her spear'.[50]

Nevertheless, Freud and H.D. covered a lot of ground in that first round of sessions. She recounted her life story – her parents, the early years of Imagism, her love for Gregg, the many traumas of the First World War, Bryher and her visionary experiences on their trip to Greece – and she kept a dream journal, which they plumbed for clues. They began to investigate 'the pure homo layer'

Sigmund Freud with chows.

of H.D.'s consciousness.[51] Bryher was excited that Freud deemed Bryher 'ONLY a boy'.[52] Like Chadwick, however, Freud could ignore the line between analyst and analysand, hosting H.D., Bryher and Perdita at his country home so that they could spend time with his new puppies. Much energy was spent in 1933, in fact, to manoeuvre gently around Freud's offer of a chow pup to their Swiss household, a grave responsibility no one wanted to take on.

It is startling to consider the stark contrast between what was happening inside Berggasse 19 and what was going on outside of Freud's flat. The day after H.D.'s third hour with Freud, Austria's parliament dissolved when the relatively inexperienced Chancellor Engelbert Dollfuss took advantage of a procedural technicality. His power was now autocratic, and he quickly worked to crush his political enemies and establish a form of fascist rule. In a time and place when each political party had its own militia, Dollfuss's action resulted in violence, as the major political parties – including the emerging Austrian Nazi party – fought in the streets. H.D. was caught up in it on more than one occasion, but to Bryher's concerns, she retorted in mid-March, 'There is no question of my leaving unless I am simply bayonet-ed out by a policeman.'[53] A week later, though, she did confide to Bryher and Kenneth how dangerous even Vienna had become: 'They simply shoot up the Jews or even people who LOOK like Jews at odd hours around the Opera, and along the Ring. Freud just says, "the world looks very, very dark for us".'[54]

In early May, 'The whole of the town was one mass of barbed wire intanglements, and stacked rifles,' but H.D. brashly headed out into the militarized zone to see an opera one night, succeeding in her quest after facing off with armed guards.[55] She was 'really very excited' about the hullabaloo: 'I must say it was marvelous, the way they were ready to shoot . . . It was magnificent. You would have loved it. Imagine the opera steps with soldiers and yet opera going on . . . if one faces the guns straight, one feels so much better and one would not mind the horrors if one believed in it all.'[56] Ever an ardent follower of politics, Bryher was not amused by H.D.'s casual tone, urging her to cut short her sessions. H.D., however, remained resolute about not interrupting her analysis until the day, 12 June, she was held on a tram while it was searched for bombs. H.D. left Vienna shortly thereafter with a nebulous plan of returning in the autumn, though she did not escape the horrors of the political situation. Bryher had turned her home into a waystation. By the end of the war, she had smuggled more than a hundred artists and analysts out of occupied territories, mostly Jews. (One notable failure was her attempt to rescue Frankfurt School theorist Walter Benjamin, who died trying to escape Vichy France.)

It is not an exaggeration to claim that H.D. was remarkably brave in this period. Amidst the political turmoil, she was nonetheless enjoying Viennese life with real gusto: its university coffeehouses, its stunning churches, its famous art museums, its opera house (where she was struck with a 'real old-time school-girl' crush on Czech opera singer Maria Jeritza[57]), even the porn shops. Bryher had become obsessed with the androgynous Austrian Jewish film star Elisabeth Bergner, whom she befriended and attempted (apparently unsuccessfully) to seduce. H.D. ventured out again and again to find 'slime poses' – sexually explicit photographs of Bergner – to send Bryher, and less explicit photos for Perdita, who shared her infatuation. (Perdita's crushes on men and women tended to follow her mothers' romantic interests.) 'I enclose some of the pictures, I finally got into the old dame's den, it was fearful, several other Lesbians buying other people . . . I blushed so,' H.D. confessed to Bryher, adding, 'I must take you there.'[58] On another venture out, 'The old dame . . . leers at me so, said if I could come in one day by appointment, she would show me some pictures of "Bergner" that she does not always show clients . . . please come and do your own whoring.'[59] On yet another trip, the shopkeeper laughs at H.D.'s request for more pictures of 'DIE Bergner??????', correcting her, 'D E R Bergner', signalling Bergner's masculinity. 'Sooooo-oo now, we know,' H.D. exclaimed to a delighted Bryher.[60]

H.D. did not go back to Vienna in the autumn of 1933. The situation there was worsening, with support for Nazism surging among the disenfranchised and poverty-stricken Austrians. Dollfuss was assassinated in July of 1934. H.D. and Bryher fretted over the safety of Freud and his family, but he scoffed at the notion that he was in danger. A number of stressors intervened, however, driving H.D. back into analysis with Freud in the autumn of 1934. Bryher's father died steadfast in an erroneous belief that it was John, not Bryher, who had the business acumen to carry out his legacy. The acrimonious settling of the estate resulted in a permanent falling out with her brother, with whom they had been close. When H.D. went to London to support Bryher, her flat was robbed by the infamous 'stiletto thief', who stole clothing, undergarments and a gift from Freud, who was himself unwell. When she learned that Freud's analysand whose hour had preceded hers had died in a plane crash, she took it as a sign. She resumed sessions in October.

In preparation, the two women had devised a coded language for their letters, which they knew would be subject to censors.[61] 'Already in Vienna, the shadows were lengthening or the tide was rising,' H.D. records in her later memoir *Tribute to Freud*, remembering 'occasional coquettish, confetti-like showers from the air, gilded paper swastikas and narrow strips of printed paper like the ones we pulled out of our Christmas bon-bons . . . One read in clear primer-book German, "Hitler gives bread", "Hitler gives work", and so on'.[62] She followed swastikas chalked on the sidewalks to Freud's door.[63] This second round of sessions only lasted for a little over a month. It was simply too dangerous to complete analysis.

Even in this short time, however, H.D. felt she made great progress in understanding her sexuality. H.D. did not always agree with Freud: 'The Professor wasn't always right,' she repeated more than once in *Tribute to Freud*. She held firmly to her spiritual beliefs, even as he derided them. During the 1933 sessions, she had been 'disturbed' when Freud dismissed her feelings about Gregg: 'When I told the Professor that I had been infatuated with Frances Josepha and might have been happy with her he said, "No – biologically, no".'[64] But in 1934, Freud seemed to have reconsidered his earlier position, concluding that 'you had two things to hide, one that you were a girl, the other that you were a boy.' As Susan Stanford Friedman has compellingly argued, Freud's views shifted on sexuality as a result of working with H.D.[65] H.D. breaks the ban on writing about her sessions to relate the news to Bryher: 'It appears that I am that all-but extinct phenomena, the perfect bi-.'[66]

For H.D., this process of psychoanalysis – of 'un-UNKing the UNK of de-bunking the junk'[67] – had significant ramifications for her work. As she explained to Bryher, 'it seems the conflict consists partly that what I write commits me – to one sex, or the other . . . I have tried to be man, or woman, but I have to be both. But it will work out, papa [Freud] says and I said, now in writing.'[68] This was a breakthrough. As Friedman observes, H.D. 'could defy Freud while revering him'.[69] Her poem 'The Master' is a tribute to this ambivalence. On the one hand, 'He was very beautiful,/ the old man,/ and I knew wisdom'.[70] His acknowledgement of her bisexuality (which may have surprised him more than it surprised her), and his insight into how it impacted her work, taught her to accept that 'I had two loves separate'.[71] But nonetheless, 'I was angry with the old man/ with his talk of the man-strength'.[72]

In her prose, one can readily discern the effects of H.D.'s analysis with Freud. Never again would she produce the sparkling, elusive, cinematic, experimental prose of the late 1920s and the 1930s. Freud decried 'dope-y stream of consciousness' and other modernist techniques as obfuscatory, deeming them barriers to a healed psyche.[73] As H.D. tells Bryher in the midst of analysis, 'the "cure" will be, I fear me, writing that damn vol. straight, as history, no frills as in Narthex, Palimp. and so on, just a straight narrative, then later, changing names and so on.'[74]

Two examples from the 1930s illustrate well Freud's influence. Emboldened by his suggestion that she, 'the perfect bi-', embodies both man and woman, H.D. summoned a character from *Kora and Ka*, John Helforth, 'to edit the works of the pre-Freud H.D.'[75] Helforth composes a preface to *Nights*, her 1931 surrealist account of twelve sequential nights with a male lover, David (based on Dan Birt). The original text is H.D.'s most sexually explicit fiction, each chapter devoted to an encounter in the narrator's bed, and its scenes include intercourse, masturbation and premature ejaculation. Helforth's first act is to kill off the narrator, Natalia, by suicide. The original novella is a fascinating exploration of the ways in which sex can break down identity, how the sex drive and the death drive intersect, and how pain and pleasure can coexist. An editor of scientific textbooks, however, Helforth pathologizes these aspects of the narrative. What had been potentially radical becomes nightmarish under his eye. While he admires her prose, he has little faith in its veracity.

A comparison of H.D.'s two verse translations of Euripides in this period, *Hippolytus Temporizes* (1927) and *Ion* (1937), is also telling, the former written before analysis, the latter after. The stories are similar: a powerful queen, a lost son and the destructive intervention of the gods. In *Hippolytus Temporizes*, the characters are doomed. The young Hippolytus is driven mad by his incestuous desire for his mother, and is tricked into consummating that desire with his stepmother, Phaedra, who brazenly expresses her lust for Hippolytus. Both die. *Ion*, however, ends not tragically but with a wholesome reconciliation between a mother and her son. As in Helforth's preface to *Nights*, a heavy-handed editorial voice intrudes on *Ion*, explicating and interpreting for the reader. It seems to have been a therapeutic exercise: 'if I get this Ion done,'

H.D. declared to Bryher, 'it will break the back-bone of my H.D. repression.'[76] Though her translation was panned by critics, it is hardly surprising that Freud found himself 'deeply mov[ed]' by *Ion*, applauding its 'victory of reason over passions'.[77]

Not just a patient but a student of Freud, H.D. was now qualified as a lay analyst, and she treated friends (rather informally). Though her perceived writer's block was not alleviated until the onset of the Second World War, she did feel stronger by the end of her sessions in Vienna, which meant that she could face both a difficult period in her relationship with Bryher and her divorce from Aldington in 1938. H.D. and Richard had long been in agreement that a divorce was unwise, as their marriage shielded her relationship with Bryher as well as his with first Arabella Yorke, then Brigit Patmore – both of whom referred to themselves publicly as 'Mrs. Aldington', to H.D.'s chagrin. Over the years, H.D. followed gossip of his romantic escapades with a mixture of amusement and pity. However, when, in 1937, he told her he had fallen in love with Patmore's young daughter-in-law and wanted to start a family with her, she was astounded but readily consented to a divorce.[78] No-fault divorce was not an option then, and the process was lengthy and arduous for H.D., who had to testify to traumatic moments in their marriage and act the part of spurned wife, a role she disliked as much as she detested the term 'mistress'. The adultery of both parties was aired in court, the ultimate blame placed, by their mutual design, on an 'over-sexed' Aldington. At least, Bryher reassured H.D., committing perjury about her relationships with Bryher and with Kenneth would go unpunished.[79] In June of 1938, the divorce was finalized, just in time for the birth of Aldington's daughter, Catha, in July.

Tensions between H.D. and Bryher heightened as the political landscape darkened across Europe, and more and more, they lived apart. Bryher monitored news of Nazism closely, talking about it incessantly to anyone who would listen. She must have felt like the ancient Cassandra by the late 1930s, her prophecies doomed to be ignored. But just as H.D. had rebuffed Aldington's attempts to ship her off to the United States during the First World War, she resented Bryher's demands that she and Perdita seek safe haven across the pond. She simply couldn't write in America, and her relative lack of productivity in the 1930s still stung. Regarding one particularly ferocious battle, she drolly describes Bryher as 'like an icicle, filled with dynamite, dressed up as a sky-scraper'.[80] Tiring of Bryher's pessimism, H.D. complained to a friend of the 'nice, happy, unique, quaint, demure, delightful, astonishing, astounding, political, poetical, botanical, snake-in-Eden-ful, Hitlers-in-his-heaven-alls-wrong-with-the-world-ful letters I get from Bryher!'[81]

Today, we would call Bryher a 'news junkie'. By the end of the decade, however, H.D. too was hooked on the news reports of Nazi atrocities and the coming war – she called news of the war 'dope' – listening compulsively to the radio Bryher sent her and reading newspaper accounts daily. 'I listen-in to everything now,' she tells Bryher, 'I seem to be turning into a military expert.'[82] The Second World War was to be as traumatic as the First for H.D. But it also rekindled her creative spirit.

6
'this is not writing, this is burning', 1939–46

The Blitz began on 7 September 1940. Until May of the following year, the bombing of London was relentless, destroying more than 1 million homes and killing more than 40,000 civilians. Londoners spent the nights in makeshift camps underground, in Tube stations. The barrage did not cease in 1941; it continued throughout the war. Nightly blackouts, noise bans and curfews were rigidly enforced for nearly six years as the British sought to impede the vision and hearing, and thus the accuracy, of German bombers. Food was meagre, rationed severely and available only to those standing in long daily queues. H.D. had survived one world war in England's capital, but she could not have anticipated how much worse the second would be. Unlike the First World War, the Second was all-encompassing for non-combatants, altering radically their everyday lives.

Certainly before 1940, there was little indication that this war would be that different, but it was unquestionable that war was imminent. H.D. and Bryher had, in fact, been waiting for it, having witnessed at first hand the rise of Nazism in Berlin and Vienna earlier in the decade. The end of 1938 had brought the violence of Kristallnacht, when Nazis vandalized and burnt down synagogues and Jewish-owned homes and businesses, lynched hundreds of Jewish Germans and committed tens of thousands to concentration camps. A couple of months later, Hitler openly called for the extermination of Jews, and by the end of 1939 Germany had occupied much of eastern Europe, including Poland. Through the first part of 1939, however, H.D. and Bryher continued to move back and forth between their London and Swiss residences. Two deaths befell them in September of 1939: Bryher's mother, Hannah Ellerman, died just weeks before Freud finally succumbed to jaw cancer. Finally free of her mother's hold on her, Bryher traipsed through Eastern Europe and Scandinavia and took flying lessons.

But life as normal was not to last much longer. As German aggression escalated, Britain and France declared war on Germany on 3 September 1939. Shortly thereafter, H.D. decided to return from Switzerland to London for the duration of the war – she felt homesick – but the process wasn't easy. She made it to England by mid-November of 1939, notifying Bryher upon arrival, 'It will take me a long time to get over the shock of the crossing.'[1] Characteristically stubborn, Bryher was still holding out hope she would be able to wait out the war in Switzerland. She had even applied to house displaced zoo animals at Kenwin.[2]

Bryher would not make it to London until nearly a year later. In the interim, H.D. and Bryher exchanged letters almost daily, discussing such topics as the German invasion of Scandinavia, the Dutch government's decampment to England, the installation of Winston Churchill as prime minister, the Battle of Dunkirk, the fall of Paris and the beginning of the Blitz. The letters are as detailed as they felt they could get away with, given the demands of censorship of information in the war era, and they reveal a depth of knowledge about the war that H.D. simply did not have – or need to have – during the First World War. 'I have felt this, as I never felt anything in the last war,' she told Bryher.[3] The quotidian shifts to the background in their correspondence, as they converse about troop movements and various kinds of weaponry, the constitutional crisis created by the surrender of Leopold III, the relative solidity of the concrete structure of H.D.'s apartment building and the rousing rhetoric of Churchill's 4 June address – 'We shall fight on the beaches, we shall fight on the landing grounds, we shall fight in the fields and in the streets, we shall fight in the hills; we shall never surrender.'

The occupation of France was particularly poignant for H.D. and her circle. 'Paris! I feel I have lost a love and a lover,' she moaned to her friend May Sarton, 'Those cities are more personal than people, Vienna, Paris, Prague.'[4] She commiserated, too, with their friend Robert Herring, who responded that France had betrayed itself: 'I'm with you – we can endure so much and so much, but when it comes to La France, one simply has to go into retreat . . . and emerge with new skin, as you say.'[5] Writing from the safety of the States, Macpherson joined the chorus: 'Today, with poor France fallen, one can remember only golden days spent there in happy love . . . England now faces its greatest and most perilous day.'[6] Churchill's stirring 16 July speech offered them hope, at least for a time: 'I proclaim my faith', he declared, 'that some of us will live to see a fourteenth of July when a liberated France will once again rejoice in her greatness and in her glory and once again stand forward as the champion of the freedom and the rights of man.'

For much of the war H.D. felt petrified, but strangely invigorated. She relished the newfound camaraderie in London, where suddenly 'everyone is so mate-y and kind, visit round on the street-corners, very continental'.[7] Friends and family were anxious to hear about her experience in London, and her responses emanate frenzied energy and intractable resolve. 'Everyone now – but everyone – is a fireman,' she boasted to a friend, as she related the story of a child who put out an incendiary with 'her little party-slippers'.[8] 'Every morning is a sort of special gift,' she reassured a concerned Marianne Moore just weeks after the Blitz began,

> a new day to be cherished and loved, a DAY that seems to love back in return . . . life should always have been like

that, the wasted days, years! Every new morning is like a
return from a bout of fever . . . and strangely I, personally
and others who have been able to stick it, seem to feel
more alive and physically stronger than for years.[9]

'The BEAUTY of life', she told Bryher, 'is unbearable'.[10]

Three weeks into the Blitz, H.D. found Bryher on her stoop,
perched atop her suitcase in a 'belligerent frame of mind'.[11] Her
crossing had been far more harrowing. The couple settled into a
life above ground during the day, and in a small storage space on
the ground floor by night, where they had set up cots.[12] Unable to
sleep through bombings, H.D. donned wax ear plugs, practised
positive visualization exercises and occasionally took barbiturates.
Eventually, fatigued in the later years of the war, they resolved
to stay in their flat at night, come what may. 'As Hilda sensibly
remarked,' Bryher recalled in her Second World War memoir *Days
of Mars*, 'If we are going to be killed, let us be comfortable up to the
last moment.'[13]

Striving for normalcy, they established a routine as best
they could. They went out most days. They took strolls in their
neighbourhood and toured old churches, wading through rubble to
take in crumbling edifices, plastic statues of bulldogs, 'the miasma
of burnt out and rotting masonry from derelict houses' and body
parts being collected by volunteer war workers.[14] H.D. was shocked
'to walk down a familiar street and look up into a facade, open
like a theatre scene – and see a room open to the sky at the top
where a friend lived, where I visited her'. She was disheartened to
see 'familiar squares with the railings torn up for scrap-iron, for
the guns, whole streets gutted, churches where one had gone in'.[15]
In the winter, they used makeshift poles to trudge through the ice
and snow.[16] They attended films and plays – war films, historical
romances, Restoration comedies, musicals, cross-dressing farces,
Shakespearean drama – having become accustomed to taking in

stride the inevitable interruptions of air raid sirens and bombs. At home, H.D. worked quietly at embroidery, while Bryher learned Farsi.

At least three times their immediate neighbourhood was bombed: once, in 1941, while H.D. was away; another time while leaving a restaurant; and again when an explosive landed in nearby Hyde Park. On another occasion, an unexploded bomb was found alarmingly close by; shaken, H.D. wrote in her memoir *The Gift*, 'We did not know the monster was there.'[17] But destruction from bombs quickly became commonplace. 'We have all had time-bombs peppered around,' H.D. recounts to Sarton, but 'they are not so bad, the danger is to the demolition squads, not to us'.[18] Bryher was proud that Londoners stayed calm and carried on: 'They walked through bombs with their shopping baskets and clustered up by the guns in the park as if it were a ball game, to applaud.'[19]

Food was scarce, and H.D. – nearly 1.83 metres (6 ft) tall – suffered perpetually from hunger and malnutrition. Bryher waited patiently in ration lines, while H.D. prepared their sparse meals. They dined almost daily at their favourite restaurant, even after a bomb had blown out its windows: 'More open than usual,' a hastily constructed sign quipped that morning to their loyal customers.[20] Care packages from the States were welcome but never enough, as were eagerly awaited regular shipments of fresh vegetables, fruit and flowers from Woodhall, the farm that H.D.'s acolyte Silvia Dobson and her family operated (with Bryher's financial help) in nearby Kent. The gift of a pineapple became the occasion for a party. Briefly, Bryher and H.D. even raised chickens in the city. Their bodies anaemic, deprived of essential vitamins, they had both lost teeth by the end of the war and were frequently ill with colds and flu. 'I KNOW that much, if not all, of the EYE trouble is lack of certain foods, nerve-condition, strain of war etc. My lower teeth have come unstuck, I look like the Witch of Endor . . . it is a gum-condition, due to lack of lemon and orange juice . . . makes me feel

90 in the shade,' H.D. wryly informed a friend.[21] By 1944, the food situation in London reached its most dire point.[22]

In the midst of it all, by fits and starts, Perdita had grown up. Her education had been haphazard and sporadic. She failed to thrive both in a dress-mending school and in acting classes taught by John Gielgud. Her friend and former au pair, Alice Modern, had turned her on to leftist and anti-Nazi activism, so, as a teen, 'Communism seemed the only rightful solution to the world problems.' 'Hitler had come to power when I was fourteen,' she points out in an unpublished memoir. Flush with the idealism of youth, she spent time hanging out in the East End with 'Fascists, Green shirts, and Communists all selling papers and wearing their badges', participating in protest marches and dreaming of a Jewish husband.[23] Perhaps not surprisingly, then, the tomboyish Perdita – whom Bryher had once described as a 'baby Amazon with black hair and assertive paws'[24] – found purpose when she embraced war work, signing on to drive a mobile canteen during the Blitz, 'right into the danger areas, with buildings crashing about her, sometimes on duty for twelve hours at a stretch, sometimes feeding hundreds of soldiers, workers and bombed-out people'.[25] Nightly, she delivered sustenance, returned to wash up the utensils and cups and then headed back out into the fray.

Perdita was not without fear, but she enjoyed the camaraderie and the drama. She wrote about her experience of the Blitz, as did H.D., who memorialized Perdita's co-worker, improbably but actually named Bunny Thunder, who was so addicted to the exhilaration that she never took a night off. Like Bryher, who viewed women in uniform as a foreshadowing of future gender equality, H.D. admired the bravery of Perdita, Bunny and their comrades-in-arms: 'such intensity and joy and vive in these girls'.[26] H.D.'s anxiety about Perdita is evident, however, in her poem 'May 1943', which memorializes a young female canteen driver, 'Goldie', who was killed in the bombing, 'found sitting upright/ at the wheel of her emergency car,/ dead'.[27] H.D. and Bryher were surely relieved when Perdita abandoned a plan to take an ambulance course.

Though she feared at times for Perdita's safety, H.D. never wavered about her own decision to remain in London, even as the situation worsened and dragged out beyond her expectations. She was loyal to the country that had first supported her artistic efforts, and she wanted to remain with her family: both Perdita and Bryher were UK citizens. 'If one has taken joy and comfort from a country,' she declared, 'one does not want to leave it when there is trouble about.'[28] Recollecting the period some years later, Perdita expressed pride in H.D.'s fortitude: 'Nobody, we might have thought, could be more unsuited to bombardment than my mother,' but 'she never mentioned her nerves. Her mornings were orderly and serene, consecrated to work.'[29] Bryher concurred, crediting H.D. for helping her get through the worst of it: 'Hilda, I knew no one braver . . . She endured the blitz stoically, refusing to go to a shelter and I remember her sitting in the hall during a raid and saying as a bomb fell particularly close, "<u>must</u> they make so much noise?"'[30]

News of Nazi atrocities had impelled H.D. to set aside her pacifism, for 'the world can't continue with that band of ill-bred deluded barbarians about.'[31] In an open letter to Bryn Mawr alumnae, she urged the United States to enter the fray, warning against the dictatorship Hitler would establish should Germany win the war, and the subsequent economic impact of Germany's interference with American trade with Europe. She shuddered at the idea of a generation of young Americans under German rule, and foresaw an obliteration of rational and reasoned government.[32] Thus, when Pearl Harbor was bombed on 7 December 1941, H.D. was 'excited and stimulated' that the United States would at last enter the war.[33] Her view of the war was nuanced. She saw with clarity that the Nazis had to be stopped, but she was unwilling to absolve the Allied countries: 'though we take our place beside the legions of Light, we must never forget how each one of us (through inertia, through indifference, through ignorance) is, in part, responsible for the world-calamity.'[34]

Unaccustomed to extended periods together in such a tight space – 'close quarters for two such turbulent spirits', Perdita astutely observed[35] – and worn down by the relentless stress of constant bombardment, Bryher and H.D. did grow weary over the course of the war years. Trauma begat trauma begat trauma. 'It's not just this raid . . . it's remembering all the others,' H.D. explained.[36] They mourned the surrender of Greece in 1941, lamented Virginia Woolf's suicide and wept over their old friend Violet Hunt when she died the following year. Their close friend Gerald Henderson lost an eye when his flat was bombed; other friends lost their homes; and H.D.'s long-time friend George Plank never recovered from war-related illness.[37] They were stricken to learn of the internment at Vittel of their dear friends Sylvia Beach and Adrienne Monnier. They fretted about the plight of children in occupied Europe, and Bryher was still trying to help Jewish orphans immigrate to the UK at war's end. By 1944, they felt increasingly desperate. The mood in London seesawed: while the Allied forces turned the tide, the Germans, realizing impending loss, ramped up their bombing campaign with new 'doodlebug' missiles.

Throughout the war, H.D.'s sole complaint was about the relentless noise – of bombs, air raid sirens, ambulances and the telephone, and the clatter of a regular stream of houseguests to whom they offered temporary succour at their Lowndes Square flat. There was already a 'Lowndes Group' forming when Bryher finally made it to London,[38] but once there she turned their home into a 'sort of telephone-booth or box or post-office counter or medical consulting clinic'.[39] For Bryher, it was not the noise but the confinement that chafed. Her rescue work was curtailed due to the French occupation, and she longed for action and purpose. But friends bolstered their spirits. The Dobsons, Herring, Plank, Edith and Osbert Sitwell and the novelist Elizabeth Bowen (who was then working for the Ministry of Information) bustled in and out of their flat.

For H.D., intensive reading about the occult and regular participation in séances offered a quieter comfort, as well as creative inspiration. After her difficult breakup with Macpherson in the early 1930s, and her concomitant battle with writer's block, she had expanded her reading in astrology, Tarot, palmistry, even fortune-telling. Seeking an alternative perspective to reorient herself and her writing, she began to read occult lore as well, mostly Westernized versions of Eastern religion and mysticism. She was impressed with the Curtiss books – a series of volumes based loosely in theosophy, co-authored by an American couple – which spoke of the end of the hypermasculine Piscean Age and the coming of the Aquarian Age, a millennium of women's empowerment and pacifism. 'Women, WOMAN', she wrote excitedly to Sarton, 'this new Aquarian age we have been told is well on the way – a woman's age, in a new sense of WOMAN.'[40] The heroism of her daughter and Bunny Thunder was but one example of what such a future might hold.

In late autumn 1941, H.D. wandered into the International Institute for Psychic Investigation, a few blocks from her flat. Drawn in, she attended lectures and browsed their library. It was there at Walton House that she met Arthur Bhaduri, an Anglo-Indian medium who, with his mother and Bryher, conducted regular séances with H.D. for much of the war. Bryher, too, sought out a medium, one Mr Redmond, who, as Havelock Ellis had decades earlier, confirmed her view of gender: 'You look at people not as men or women but as souls, you do not see them belonging to the sexes.'[41]

In the autumn of 1943, H.D. heard Hugh Dowding lecture on his own psychic research. Lord Dowding had been air chief marshal during the Battle of Britain, and H.D. was quite taken with his turn to spiritualism. That an image of wings had surfaced in a séance with Bhaduri only strengthened her desire to contact him. So commenced a correspondence and series of meetings between the two, but her efforts to join his circle and to procure validation of her own spiritualist experiences were unsuccessful. H.D. expressed disappointment about his books on the subject, but she found Dowding attractive and admired his sincerity. His final repudiation of her spiritualist work in 1946 would feature in her prose work in the years to come.

Occasional excursions were crucial to H.D.'s and Bryher's mental and physical well-being. The two had considered but rejected a plan to live in Cambridge, though they took refuge there on odd weekends. When they needed a break, they braved overcrowded trains to head north to Derbyshire, to see Edith and Osbert Sitwell at Renishaw Hall, or Robert Herring, whose temporary wartime lodgings were nearby. A gay writer and editor, and a friend of Kenneth Macpherson's, Herring had joined their ménage in the late 1920s, and he had co-starred in *Borderline*. H.D. and Bryher helped him redecorate his family home in Eckington with items raided from the Ellerman storage unit in Battersea in January of 1941. 'Can anything more depressing be imagined than driving through war-London, to a warehouse in order to sift over a mid-Victorian past?' H.D. wrote in her account of the Blitz, *Within the Walls*, but the two had rather enjoyed selecting ostentatious and campy paintings and decor for Herring.[42]

Bryher, as usual, was always on the go. She summered in Cornwall – for 'a few weeks in the salt air far from the charred smells of London'[43] – at the Trenoweth Valley Flower Farm she had helped her closest school friend, Doris Long, purchase. At least once she travelled to Scotland, having befriended two of Norman Douglas's entourage: the novelist Sir Compton Mackenzie, whose lesbian novel *Extraordinary Women* had attracted H.D.'s attention, and his wife, Faith, an author in her own right. Though she did not travel as frequently, H.D. accompanied Bryher to Cornwall or went to Woodhall for a month each summer. Woodhall's farmhouse was rustic, boisterous and cramped, and the work was strenuous, but H.D. soaked in the country air and the natural setting – the forests, the fields and the flowers – and fantasized about a home of her own there (though her scheme failed to convince Bryher). Missing international travel, they were heartened to hear a polyphony of languages in the streets of London – French, Polish, Dutch, Norwegian – to view Russian films and war shorts and to listen to French, German and Italian spoken on *London Calling Europe*, a bbc programme in which British citizens reached out to denizens of Nazi-occupied countries.[44]

By the end of the war, conscription in the uk was compulsory for men and women under fifty. By 1943, over 80 per cent of the women in the uk worked outside the home. Princess Elizabeth trained as a mechanic and driver during the war, and Churchill's daughters served: Diana in the Women's Royal Naval Service, Sarah as an interpreter in the Women's Auxiliary Air Force, and Mary in the Women's Voluntary Service and the Auxiliary Territorial Service. Perdita moved on from canteen driver to a job in the oss at Bletchley Park, and engaged in 'Counter espionage, Very Cloak and Dagger at the higher echelon'.[45] 'Higher echelon' indeed: Bletchley Park was the centre of Allied code-breaking efforts during the war, the site of the 'Turing Machine'. Her family were permitted to know very little about her work: Perdita's 'dept. deals in hush-hush what-not – she is very secretive about it, but anyhow, we do know, they are utilizing her languages', H.D. confided to her friend Viola Jordan.[46] Bryher's lessons in French and German had paid off.

While Perdita and Bryher found ways to contribute to the war effort, H.D. was in her fifties, too old to participate – a fact that nagged at her. 'It is terribly difficult for people . . . to be in war and not at war,' she protested to Sarton.[47] She registered as a therapist in London – her work with Freud qualified her as a lay analyst – but she was never called to offer aid.[48] She also helped out at the office of *Life and Letters Today*, the journal Bryher co-edited with Herring, having acquired it two years after *Close Up* had ceased publication in 1933. It was a successful venture. Under their leadership, the journal widened its range to include not just British but American and Asian writers, and to publish work on film as well as literature. Unlike other modernist serials, the journal enjoyed a wide circulation.

Most of H.D.'s 'war work' came in the form of a return to her writing. As H.D. waited by her radio through the 'Phoney War', she had found herself unable to write, or even read anything erudite. Rather, she indulged in 'intensive trash-reading', mystery novels, police procedurals and the occasional lesbian romance.[49] But once the war arrived at her doorstep, H.D.'s imagination was ignited by the drama around her, and her 1930s struggles with writer's block ended abruptly. 'This age, if we live to see it, will be the most interesting in world history, I think,' she told her uncle Clifford Howard.[50] She began writing when the bombs began to fall, documenting the terror she believed only the magic spell of words could dispel, but also the tenacity of non-combatants, who reimagined the sound of bombs as heavy snow, their lights as chandeliers. She revisited and revised old manuscripts, attempting again to place *Pilate's Wife*; finishing up a draft of *Bid Me to Live*, her final *roman-à-clef* of the First World War years; and preparing the first part of *Tribute to Freud* (from her notes on their sessions) for publication in *Life and Letters Today*. And she composed new works: three long poems and the prose sketches *Within the Walls* about the Blitz; *Majic Ring*, an account of her experiments in occultism and spiritualism; the autobiographical novel *The Gift*; and her epic tripartite poem, *Trilogy*.

Norman Holmes Pearson – an American OSS agent who would go on to become a Yale professor of English and founder of American studies, as well as H.D.'s literary executor – was instrumental in encouraging H.D., and Bryher, to begin writing during the war. Pearson studied literature at Yale and then

Oxford, where writer and spy Donald Downes recruited him into intelligence work. H.D. had met him at Kenneth's apartment in New York on one of her visits in the late 1930s. They reconnected in London during the war and, with Bryher, enjoyed regular Sunday meals together at Lowndes Square.

A chief focus of Pearson's academic career would be the establishment of the significance of American modernism. Inspired by the war, fortified by Bryher and Pearson's support, H.D. returned to her typewriter, even late into the evenings after noise and light was forbidden, even when she was sternly reprimanded for breaking ordinances. Fearing that she 'might not be able to bear witness to this truth', because '[she] might be annihilated', she feverishly recorded her experience and insights.[51] She worried over the need to preserve old manuscripts, too: 'if I am blitzed, the house will go with me and the stack of papers will go, too,' she reasoned, but 'If I am not blitzed, of course it may be interesting.'[52]

H.D.'s interest in politics, culture and the arts revived, and she was not alone: 'a new phase' had begun, she thought, in which 'people are taking concerts, "art" in general very seriously, piously, you might say,' citing queues of unprecedented length at the National Gallery.[53] When she was asked to participate, with T. S. Eliot and other poets, in a reading to aid French refugees, she surprised everyone by consenting. Draped in an elegant black dress that cost the family an astonishing number of ration coupons, she read 'Ancient Wisdom Speaks' with the queen mother, Princess Margaret, and the future Queen Elizabeth in attendance at Aeolian Hall, where the BBC had just been forced to relocate after their offices were bombed. A revival in the arts was a salve for the pain of the British 'Books for Battle' programme, which burned books for fuel and recycled paper into gun cartridge cases. Though the effort was voluntary, participation was coerced, according to the historian Peter Thorsheim: 'If people were not sufficiently generous, officials warned, they would use the wartime powers Parliament had granted them to seize private property.'[54] She and Bryher contributed, but book burning, she would write in *Trilogy*, was 'the most perverse gesture'.[55]

In the early days of the war, H.D. began *The Gift*, an autobiographically based *Künstlerroman*. *The Gift* explores myriad forms of art-making in her early life, as she and her brothers re-enacted theatrical dramas they had witnessed, crafted elaborate manger scenes for Christmas and drew in their sketchbooks. To the children, even her father's microscope was a magical device, exposing the presence of another world, invisible to the eye.

But *The Gift*, too, coalesced some of the ideas about temporality that she had been pondering in her various metaphysical pursuits but were now catalysed by the war. The British ban on photography during the war created a curious 'gap in time' that H.D. felt could not be filled. Moreover, the war 'cracked open old tombs for most of us'. She was confronted with 'child-memories blasted up, as it were, by the bombs'.[56] So rich is the material on the Moravian community in which she was raised that it is easy to ignore the Blitz scenes that periodically erupt in the volume, but H.D. was insistent that they were key to understanding the book. When she mailed the manuscript to the States, she learned that British censors had mutilated those scenes. 'The whole point of the book was lost,' she wailed, 'the subtlety and point of the link-up with shock at age of 10 and shock at age of 55 (circa) was lost'.[57]

The Gift transforms her family's musical 'gifts' into a psychic gift that allowed her to see a collapsing of historical and present time – the early encounters of the newly arrived Moravians with Indians in colonial America, and H.D.'s Moravian childhood. This duality is reflected in the book's structure, which parallels these periods with contemporaneous scenes of London during the Second World War. A harrowing account of a burning girl at the book's opening foretells a present fate: 'the whole structure of civilisation may go down at any moment like the Christmas-tree in the Seminary that

caught fire when the girl in the crinoline was burnt to death.'[58]
Late nineteenth-century Moravians haunted by tales of Indian
massacres found their parallel in the buildings set aflame in
modern-day London.

In the early 1940s, then, she is beginning to complicate
the palimpsest motif that had been a hallmark of her writing.
Palimpsest refers to writing and rewriting on the same surface,
such that traces of the past are still visible in the present day.
Now she was conceptualizing history as folding back on itself,
collapsing and expanding like an accordion, so that two epochs
could meet. During the Blitz, humans constantly faced their
mortality, and under such conditions 'we become time-less and are
impersonalized because in fact we are all really one of thousands
and thousands who are equally facing a fact, the possibility, at any
given second, of complete physical annihilation.'[59] This is because,
H.D. hypothesized, the Blitz caused a rift in ordinary temporality
such that she could exist 'in both dimensions at the same time',
the 'ordinary world' and the '4th dimensional world, the world of
dream, of vision'.[60]

This theory of temporality met the very real concerns of a
middle-aged non-combatant who wished to turn writing into
meaningful war work. It undergirds *Trilogy*, one of her best-known
works. In the three poems that comprise this epic, H.D. is excavator
of the ruins of history, pushing back further than ancient Greece
and Rome – sites so well known in her previous poetry and prose –
to explore ancient Egypt and Mesopotamia, suggesting ultimately
that the recovery and re-valuation of female deities and feminine
sensibilities is critical to rebuilding a war-torn civilization and
imagining a world averse to future warfare. The poet, as keeper and
disseminator of cultural memory in a time of violence, is essential
to the creation of this new world.

A poem of such grand design and ambition was not, could not
be, Imagist. The world stage in the early 1940s – a world in which

'The actual fire has raged round the crystal' – demanded an epic.
'The crystalline poetry to be projected, must of necessity, have
that fire in it,' H.D. reflected at the end of the decade.[61] Even as this
poem delved more deeply into the past than her previous work, it
spoke clearly to the present as well. H.D. had long scoffed at the
whole notion that her earlier work was escapist. She had always
sought truths about the contemporary world in its history. For
H.D., in fact, writers who are blind to the past are complicit in
imperialist and violent acts. 'Were it not for men's thoughts and
dreams . . . there would have been no war,' the poet Robert Duncan
would observe decades later in his extended response to *Trilogy*:
'The realization, once it is there, never ceases to trouble H.D.'[62] She
was determined to heal a cultural amnesia that she believed fatal to
civilization.

The poem took time to percolate. The seeds of *Trilogy* might well
be located in her reading and writings about Egypt in the 1920s. In
January 1942, she had 'nostalgic feelings for SAND and a different
sort of sea – it goes back partly to Egypt . . . at the opening of the
tomb.'[63] But in 1941, the idea for the poem had already begun to
coalesce, after learning of a 'little shrine' that was 'an empty shell',
burned out but 'the walls were standing'.[64] This image would frame
powerfully the first poem, *The Walls Do Not Fall*:

> ruin opens
> the tomb, the temple; enter,
> there as here, there are no doors:
>
> the shrine lies open to the sky.[65]

By May 1942, she is writing bits of verse 'in an angry midnight
frame of mind', and by late summer of that year, she is
workshopping a draft with her friend Molly Hughes, a writer and
educator who was open to H.D.'s esoteric investigations.[66] Her

reading in the occult was beginning to intersect with her reading about Egypt: 'I had read somewhere, that ANCIENT EGYPT had the germs of the original Atlantis lore and mystery,' and that Europeans had been at Atlantis as well.[67] By the end of 1943, she was ready to tell Norman Holmes Pearson about it.

The Walls Do Not Fall opens in London but moves quickly to another site of destruction, Pompeii, and then to ancient Egypt and the Middle East. She tells a cyclical story of the invasion and conquering of civilizations, the colonizing of their denizens and the replacement of their deities with those of the conqueror: 'charms are not . . . grace', they are told as their amulets were 'snatched off'.[68] As history progresses, goddesses begin to disappear, so H.D. names them – Isis, Aset, Astarte, Serqet – invoking their presence in the face of devastation wrought by masculinist aims and ambitions.

The poem also ruminates on the role of poets in war. If colonizers attempt to erase cultural memory, poets must remember. Poets are 'bearers of the secret wisdom', who choose pen over sword.[69] In *Within the Walls*, H.D. had imagined herself a corpse. Here, in *Trilogy*, war is represented as a fiery baptism, an occasion for rebirth, 'self-out-of-self'.[70] 'The bone-frame was made for/ no such shock knit within terror', but though flesh burns away, 'the skeleton stood up to it'.[71] Words, everyday objects, amulets, hold power. Fragile creatures – snails, molluscs, worms – show persistence and strength in the face of the terrors of earthly existence. Perhaps apocalypse is necessary in a world so fallen. The worm 'spin[s] [its] own shroud',[72] transmogrifying into a butterfly. The phoenix rises from the ashes.

Dated 1942, written 'in the fiery furnace', *The Walls Do Not Fall* was published by Oxford University Press in 1944.[73] Some, like Vita Sackville-West – who praised her sophisticated insight into 'the dependence of the sword on the word' – were enthusiastic about it.[74] Others were less kind. In response to a review in the *Times*

Literary Supplement, H.D. complained, rightly, that 'They had to sniff a bit because our old H.D. had not stayed "pure Greek". Why one must write at <u>60</u> (or near 60) what one wrote at 16, must remain a mystery!'[75] It was the old problem. Undaunted, however, in May of that same year, she wrote a companion piece, *Tribute to the Angels*, a 'peace poem', she told her friends. By the time it was published in 1945, she had already finished the third and final poem, *The Flowering of the Rod*, which came out in 1946.

H.D. ends *The Walls Do Not Fall* in uncertainty: '*possibly we will reach haven,/ heaven*'.[76] The second and third poems are more optimistic: 'resurrection is a sense of direction'.[77] Petitioning angels to aid her in the midst of an apocalyptic maelstrom, the speaker of *Tribute to the Angels* conjures the 'Lady', a manifestation of the divine feminine, in an alchemist's bowl. The Lady is cleansed and redeemed of her scandalous and hypersexualized representations, indications of strategies employed to disempower female deities. Venery, by the magic of alchemy, becomes veneration.[78] She carries an empty book, a 'Book of Life', in which a new world can be birthed. Leaving behind a 'smouldering' civilization, H.D. re-envisions the birth of Jesus from Mary's perspective, in *The Flowering of the Rod*.[79] The Lady takes the form of the two Marys: both Mary, mother of God, and Mary Magdalene, 'who was naturally reviled'.[80] To obtain the healing myrrh as a gift for the coming birth, this composite Mary intercepts Kaspar, one of the three wise men, who, at the sight of her, has a vision that grants him the gift of memory. He, too, can now see the past unrolled before him.

In *Trilogy*, completed in December 1944, H.D. foresees an end of war, but in London of 1944 that end was elusive. She and Bryher rejoiced at the liberation of France in late summer of that year, a landmark particularly poignant for H.D. since 'it was to France I first went from USA . . . it is something special and regenerating.'[81] But 'one wonders', she asks Sarton, 'when London will be liberated???????????'[82] They would have to persevere for almost another year. Tired of waiting, they began celebrating in April 1945, ahead of Victory in Europe Day. They jettisoned their blackout curtains, hung U.S., British and Greek flags in their windows, and slept bathed in newly lit London nights. H.D., Bryher and Herring took a restorative trip to Stratford to join in the processional for Shakespeare's birthday, revelling in 'a unity of joy' with a flood of others desperate for war's end.[83] H.D. returned soon after to spend a memorable summer in Stratford, studying the flora of Shakespeare's garden, reading Elizabethan verse in tea shops, attending plays and dreaming of a home there. These trips would inspire *By Avon River*, a volume about Shakespeare and his contemporaries.

In her poem 'Christmas 1943', H.D. observes, 'We are dizzy and a little mad', for 'we have had/ experience of a world beyond our sphere'.[84] Low levels of mental health during the war had been anticipated, but the assumption was wrong: Londoners were healthier psychologically during the war than before it. When it was over, however, mental health levels plummeted. What we now term 'post-traumatic stress disorder' had set in. As H.D. confided to her cousin, 'many of our London friends have broken down in various forms of nervous reaction, since V.E. Day'.[85] 'Saturated with old miseries', H.D. was among those struggling to transition back into normal life.[86] Even while she was eagerly making plans to deliver an invited series of lectures on English poetry at Bryn Mawr in the spring of 1946, she was suffering from exhaustion, anxiety, malnutrition, depression and illness. She was unable to make the trip to her alma mater. After several months of witnessing H.D. in this state, Bryher – in consultation with their dear friend, the psychoanalyst Walter Schmideberg – had H.D. airlifted to Switzerland, where she would live for the rest of her life, never to return to her beloved England.

7

'content, besieged with memories, like low-swarming bees', 1946–61

There is a sense in which H.D. never fully recovered from the Second World War. Six years of psychic and physical trauma aged her well beyond her years. But this did not mean that she was not joyful and productive in the post-war phase of her life. In fact, she was enormously prolific. She believed that illness, infirmity and convalescence stimulated spiritual vision, and this vision was essential to her writing.[1] Though she spent more time away from her family and friends in the last decade and a half of life – she could no longer flit back and forth between cityscape and countryside – she had a lifetime of memories on which to draw for inspiration. The flirtations of her younger years were re-created in her vivid imagination. She became consumed with memory at the very moment of life when memory, inevitably, begins to slip away. Norman Holmes Pearson – who had become her agent, her literary confidante and her 'Chevalier' – urged her along, prompting a flurry of memoirs and reflections on her life and career. Increasingly aware of the unreliability and malleability of memory, she incorporated these insights into her writings, producing some of the most nuanced work in her oeuvre.

It was in the last fifteen years of her life, too, that she embraced Switzerland as her permanent home, though the first year there after the war was challenging. On 14 May 1946, H.D. arrived at Klinik Brunner in Küsnacht, Zurich, ill, malnourished and depressed. Her symptoms – which also included anxiety and delusions – were in part the result of post-war exhaustion and meningitis, and quite probably in part, ironically, side effects of the drug that had been prescribed to treat them, sodium amytal. She seemed to improve over the summer but then apparently relapsed. By September, she was furious about being confined against her will. Alone in the facility without family or friends, subject to electro-shock and other non-consensual medical treatments, she vented her anger and terror to Bryher in letters written in pencil, because typewriters and pens weren't permitted. As H.D. began to recover, it was clear to both women that though they would remain the closest of friends, another casualty of the war would be their romantic relationship. Years of living in close quarters under tremendous strain, and a breach of trust over H.D.'s hospitalization, had taken an irreversible toll.

When she left the Klinik in November, H.D. settled in a hotel in Lausanne on Lake Léman (or Lake Geneva), a city with dozens of museums, ancient Roman ruins and beautiful churches. It was a town with a literary past: T. S. Eliot, Ernest Hemingway, Percy Shelley and a host of other writers had come to its shores before her. Living minutes away from Bryher, she was able to see her often while still maintaining her newfound independence. Immediately, H.D. established a new migratory pattern that was ideal for her writing – alternating between Lausanne and Lugano, on the Italian border, another scenic lakeside town with vibrant markets and festivals. Lugano was also a quick bus ride to the secluded home of Herman Hesse, a writer whom H.D. admired and befriended. But without the hubbub of London, her English friends falling away as the war receded into the past, she was essentially alone, and writing became her chief occupation. Her fruitful period of the war years had not come to an end, and at sixty years of age she still had another book-length epic poem, four novels, several memoirs and a diary, a book of poetry and literary history, and a series of long poems left to write. When she wasn't writing, she was reading in English, French, Italian and German.

Even before she arrived at Klinik Brunner, H.D. had begun her next book, part poetry and part prose, which she later christened *By Avon River*. Inspired by her Shakespeare Day pilgrimage and her summer in Stratford in 1945, she had penned a tripartite poem, 'Good Frend', about Claribel, a 'lost' character in Shakespeare's *The Tempest* who does not appear in the play but whose wedding to the king of Tunis is the occasion for Alonso's ship setting sail within reach of Prospero's grasp. The poem locates the play within its historical contexts – the 1609 shipwreck of the *Sea Venture* in Bermuda and the arranged marriage of Elizabeth, daughter of James I – and imagines Claribel's life. Calling on the healing power of rosemary to restore our memory, the speaker offers Claribel the voice Shakespeare had denied her: 'I only threw a shadow/ On his page,' Claribel remembers, recalling the moment of her birth when his quill 'fell/ Upon the unblotted line' and inscribed her name. Once brought to life, 'I live forever,' she declares.[2] 'Good Frend' culminates, then, in the liberation of Claribel from her author's

Bryher and H.D., 1960.

control, setting her free to wander Venice, to work side by side with the Franciscan Order of the Poor Clares and to offer succour to a fallen soldier.

Opening 'Remembering Shakespeare always, but remembering him differently,' the second part of the book was composed at the Klinik.[3] It made good use of H.D.'s notes for the lecture series she would not be able to offer at Bryn Mawr. She had been excited about the opportunity to return to her alma mater, reading and rereading the English canon, writing to friends for their advice on their favourite English lyric poems and consulting with her friend, the educator Molly Hughes, about teaching tips. Now, however, she began to transform her notes into an extended analysis of the late medieval and early modern period. 'The Guest' interweaves her commentary on the poetry of Shakespeare's contemporaries, a literary history of England and the perspective of an ageing Shakespeare suffering memory loss. H.D. sketches out a literary lineage that displaces Shakespeare to make room for other poets of his epoch, even while it pays homage to his legacy. She lauds, she indicts. As she reads generously from the works of dozens of his contemporaries, the meandering thoughts of an elderly Shakespeare facing the end of his career intrude upon her lecture and vie for space devoted to other deserving poets.

The tome filled H.D. with joy: '*Avon* is the first book that really made me happy,' she wrote to her friend George Plank.[4] Pearson was delighted with the book, and shopped it to Macmillan, who published it in 1949. A German-language edition followed in 1955, translated by a war refugee, Johannes Urzidil, who was grateful to Bryher for rescuing him and his family from what was then Nazi-occupied Czechoslovakia in 1939. H.D. boasted to Bryher that the book was 'fool-proof' in terms of popular interest, and she was right.[5] *By Avon River* was her first and only book with real crossover appeal. It was widely reviewed, overwhelmingly positively, in mainstream newspapers across the United States.

For H.D., *By Avon River* marked the beginning of a new phase of writing, a definitive end to the short lyrics of Imagism and a move towards more dynamic verse and prose, and topics both more historically aware and more reflective of her lifelong spiritual quest. It would prove to be a tremendously fertile and rewarding final phase to a career that would stretch into nearly five decades. With this, her first post-war book, she enthused, 'I had crossed literally my Rubicon, albeit AVON y-clept!'[6] Following on its heels were three works of historical fiction. It was a genre she knew well, being an avid reader of historical novels and having penned several works set in ancient Greece and Palestine in the 1920s. But these post-war writings were different, centred around more modern times in European history. Her prose work of the 1920s had used imperialism as a ready metaphor for the male domination of women in heterosexual relationships. Having survived the war, she was now interested in the origins of the current geopolitical landscape. Reviving her friendship with her former husband, Richard Aldington, she used him as a sounding board and ad hoc research assistant, and their regular and amicable correspondence continued throughout the rest of her life.

H.D. typically wrote prose under a range of pseudonyms, and she insisted that this series of three books be signed Delia Alton, her 'nom de guerre'.[7] Born in the crucible of war, 'Delia' was a name that recalled both Delos, the birthplace of Artemis and Apollo, and Delphi, site of the legendary oracle. It was Delia's vision that would dominate her work of the late 1940s. The first novel, completed in 1947, was the most ambitious, *The Sword Went Out to Sea (Synthesis of a Dream)*. Blending multiple genres – fairy tale, ghost story, science fiction, historical fiction, spiritual autobiography – the two-part novel contemplates the theatrical nature of seeming reality and the relativity of time, employing several embedded narrative frames and an unreliable narrator. The book's first part bridges autobiographically based memories of the First and Second World

Wars, exposing a recurrent war cycle perpetuated by a civilization wracked by cultural amnesia and devoted to a hypermasculinity that explicitly renounces women's values and contributions. It records Delia's experiences with spiritualism as a way of understanding how a war could create a rift in time, a split between the 'clock-time' of the material world and the 'dream-time' of another plane of existence. The structure of the second part reflects the accordion-pleated notion of time H.D. had been formulating in the war years. An astral body of Delia travels to a range of historical places and periods – some ancient, some modern – living and reliving the trauma of war. In conveying Delia's experience, H.D. reveals how the personal and the political overlap, how the realm of the private sphere radically informs social and political realities.

Her second post-war novel, completed in 1948, fictionalizes the story of Pre-Raphaelites William Morris, Dante Gabriel Rossetti and Rossetti's wife, Elizabeth Siddall. H.D. immersed herself in reading about these figures, intent on resurrecting the tragic Siddall, whose life ended in suicide, within the historical contexts of the Sepoy Rebellion of 1857 in India and the Crimean War. In this book, H.D. is interested in exploring how the woman's body serves as metaphor for conquered and colonized land, uncovering its objectification in the history of Western art. Siddall had been an artist's model before she became an artist, and H.D. captures her dissatisfaction with her treatment by the men in her circle, artistically and materially. If *Sword* was 'the crown of her achievement, her achievement itself', *White Rose and the Red* was 'a labour of love'.[8]

The last of the three, *The Mystery*, returned to the Moravian history plumbed in *The Gift*. Set in eighteenth-century Prague, the novel features a young Moravian woman and her brother, who are trying to piece together their family's past. An encounter with a magician-priest whose astral body visits other places and times becomes a vehicle for a meeting with Count Zinzendorf, the founder of Moravianism. Here it is the French Revolution that serves as historical backdrop for the action of the narrative. This was the final Delia Alton novel for H.D., who later crossed out Alton's name on the title page and pencilled in 'H.D.' instead. As she remarked to Pearson, the short novel represented 'FINIS . . . to a whole processus or life-time of experience'.[9]

H.D. was unsuccessful placing any of these historical novels with publishers – they were far different from anything she had yet attempted – but now that Pearson was collecting her papers for posterity, she was content for them to be placed on her 'shelf' at Yale. In his efforts to promote American modernism, Pearson cultivated friendships with H.D., Ezra Pound and a number of others, building ultimately an impressive archive at Yale University. To this end, he urged H.D. to compose memoirs about her modernist comrades (particularly men who were already well on the way to canonization, like Pound and Lawrence), and to organize her papers and reflect on her life's work. H.D. was not being manipulated. She was as interested in her legacy as Pearson was. Not surprisingly, then, it is *Bid Me to Live* – the fictionalized retelling of her trials during the First World War, which places D. H. Lawrence at the centre – that would be the version of that period of her life to make it into print. Drafted in 1939, the book came out in 1960 with Grove Press, garnering praise from reviewers and a nasty letter from her old friend John Cournos, who was still, after all of these years, protective of Arabella Yorke, whose affair with H.D.'s husband had ended her marriage to Aldington. It was H.D.'s fourth and final (extant) novel about her young adult years, a 'FINIS to the whole Bloomsbury episode'.[10]

For the most part, H.D.'s final decade and a half was a happy time. But she was stunned and saddened to learn of the death of Frances Gregg years after it had occurred. Having taken a job at the Navy, Army and Air Force Institute in Devonport during the war, Frances, along with her mother and her daughter, were killed in a Plymouth air raid on 21 April 1941, their house, fatefully, the only one struck on their street. Her son, Oliver, had to identify her mutilated body, among many others, on a conveyor belt.[11] It laid to rest an important chapter of H.D.'s life. Nearly all of the Greggs' belongings were destroyed by the bomb, but, fortuitously, Oliver located among her effects Pound's book of poems to H.D. – penned in the early Pennsylvania years – which H.D. had given Frances for safekeeping. It was later published with H.D.'s memoir *End to Torment*.

In 1950, H.D. and Bryher were surprised to hear from Perdita that she was engaged to be married. When the war had ended, so had Perdita's work for the OSS. After completing an improbable stint at the 'DuBarry Success School'[12] – a 'charm school' that trained women in the social graces, even as it encouraged dieting and imparted beauty tips – Perdita had found herself studying stenography in New York at the Moon Secretarial School, a place Bryher deemed suitable. Within a few months, however, Perdita confided to H.D. that she had secretly begun taking creative writing classes at Columbia University, but 'DON'T TELL FIDO just yet'.[13] Perdita, like her mothers, had found her passion in writing. She had also landed a job with literary agent John Schaffner, the man who would become her husband on 24 June 1950. A former English teacher, Schaffner worked for *Collier's* and *Good Housekeeping* magazines before founding his own agency in 1948, and he hired Perdita, unpaid, as his assistant. He would go on to represent many prominent authors, including Maxine Hong Kingston and Ray Bradbury.

Wedding plans were thrown together so quickly that it was not feasible for H.D. or Bryher to attend, so Pearson gave away the bride in a ceremony in Maine so 'over-conventional' that it shocked both of her mothers.[14] Perdita was bemused by all of the ado, in a letter to H.D.:

as you can imagine, it was quite difficult getting my parentage
all sorted out and worked into society column language . . .
The poor Society Editor got so upset; she wanted to know who
and where <u>Mr.</u> Bryher was . . . The Society Editor of the Times
and Tribune also interviewed us on the office phone, equally
baffled – and what terrifying ladies they are, so very, very snooty
and society . . . Now I can't decide whether it is Mrs. Aldington
or Mrs. Bryher who announces the wedding . . . I've asked
Fido to discuss the problem of <u>which</u> mother with you. I think
it would be fun to have you both, announcing it together![15]

What was more, Perdita informed them, she was pregnant, so it
made sense to wait to make the trip across the pond. Valentine
Schaffner was born 21 February 1951, and they flew over to meet
their first grandchild and, for the first time, their son-in-law,
to whom they quickly warmed. They were able to spend more
time with the new mother and son at Kenwin that fall, and H.D.
periodically entertained the notion of moving to New York City
near the Schaffners. Having inherited Bryher's boundless energy,
Perdita was happily settling into a life of motherhood, literary
pursuits, frequent travel and charity work.

By the early 1950s, H.D., too, was brimming with energy.
The completion of *The Mystery* in 1951 ended for H.D. an
explosion of prose in the late 1940s, a prolonged period in which,
uncharacteristically, she had not felt like writing verse at all. After
the 'overwhelming drive' to complete the Delia Alton novels,
however, 'H.D.' re-emerged: 'there was still the poetry, I discovered
to my surprise.'[16] It was research for *The Mystery* into books by
E. M. Butler – *Fortunes of Faust* and *Silver Wings* primarily – that
'struck the spark'.[17] Another 'spark' was likely the publication of
photographs of the aftermath of the U.S. bombing of Hiroshima, as
Elizabeth Willis contends, for H.D. was still concerned about the
devastation of war, and the stories we tell about it.[18] *Helen in Egypt*

arose, too, from her lifelong fascination with the figure of Helen – who shared her name with H.D.'s mother – as the cause of the legendary war between Greece and Troy.

H.D. began her second epic poem in September of 1952, coming back to the pages of Euripides after a long hiatus. Like *Trilogy*, *Helen* was a return to Egypt, but also a return to 'difficult and metaphysical' subjects in a tripartite form, 'a sort of controlled free verse' that relied on internal rhyme and a rhythm that suggested 'the roar of the chargers' in the war.[19] Hailed as 'the most ambitious and successful long poem every written by a woman poet' by Albert Gelpi,[20] *Helen in Egypt* takes up ancient Greek stories of a Helen who never goes to Troy to engage in an adulterous romance with Paris, having been whisked away by the gods to Egypt, where King Proteus offered sanctuary. In these retellings, it is rather a double of Helen – a phantom or 'eidolon' – who went to Troy. Helen was in two places at the same time.

Helen in Egypt draws significantly on H.D.'s study of astral projection and bilocation, which had been a touchstone for her since 1920 – when she believed that she had encountered the astral double of Pieter Rodeck on board the *Borodino* – and which served as a key trope in her post-war historical fiction. While Camille Flammarion's *Death and Its Mystery* had been her guide to understanding the phenomenon, in 1952 she discovered a way to integrate astral projection, Tarot, astrology and even Freudian psychoanalysis into a rich mystical belief system when Sylvia Beach sent her French Kabbalist Robert Ambelain's *Dans l'ombre des cathédrales* (1939). She began *Helen in Egypt* soon after finishing Ambelain's book, which she annotated heavily.[21] For H.D., Ambelain articulated a way to theorize that breach between 'dream-time' and 'clock-time' which was blasted open during the Second World War. Her poem would revisit old themes – the soldier-lover, the role of women in war, the ruinous consequences of cultural amnesia – but with a different, more holistic spiritual philosophy undergirding it.

The first part of *Helen in Egypt*, 'Pallinode', finds Helen on an Egyptian shore, confronted by Achilles' fury. He threatens to attack her when he recognizes her as the cause of his demise: 'You stole the chosen, the flower/ of all-time, of all-history,/ my children, my legions', he alleges, 'for you were the ships burnt'.[22] Helen, stricken, vacillates between blaming herself and seeing the infamous arrow that pierced his heel – his only point of physical vulnerability – as evidence of the plan of the gods. She comes to the realization, however, that 'She herself is the writing,' that she is a construct: 'with his anger,/ that ember, I became/ what his accusation made me.'[23] The poem, then, is concerned principally with representation.

In the second part, 'Leuké', Helen forces herself to return to memories of the war she had attempted to blot out. H.D.'s poem does not, however, take the easy path of exonerating Helen by contrasting the 'real' Helen with her eidolon. What transpires instead is that Helen, with the aid of Theseus, must face that she is in fact both Helens, that she loved Paris once, and that she had in fact loved the war. Helen is not one Helen. She is not simply Achilles' Helen or Paris' Helen or Menelaus' Helen, but many Helens: 'there was always another and another and another;/ the rose has many petals'.[24] She is not an innocent harbouring in Egypt or the whore who started the war: she is both and neither and an endless host of others.

In the final part of the poem, 'Eidolon', Paris and Achilles fight over Helen, or, rather, their constructions of Helen. In a brilliant metacritical move, H.D.'s speaker ultimately indicts art – 'the lyre-string' – in the making of war and the making of the category of woman, an idea she had begun to grapple with in *Trilogy* but which here comes to fruition.[25] Moreover, paradoxically, war is born of love, she asserts, and love of war. She must learn to think in multiplicity, to break the binary logic that has governed Western civilization for millennia. If the Lady has to be cleansed in *Trilogy*

– venery transformed into veneration – in *Helen in Egypt* the Lady comprises a full range of aspects. To understand the self, Helen must own the shards of truth in her various representations, even while complicating those constructions.

Written in the maelstrom of world war, *Trilogy* desperately seeks certainty and stability, but *Helen in Egypt* finds no such resolution. It is about chronic suffering – not about being healed, but about a never-ending process of healing.[26] H.D. had always been leery of easy resolution, but her 1950s epic promotes a life of embracing ambiguity as a necessary condition of being. Questions pepper all three parts of the poem, as there are almost as many interrogative as declarative lines in *Helen*.

H.D. completed the sequence in 1954, and, at Pearson's request, consented to two recording sessions in January and February of 1955. It took a fair amount of convincing, but once in the studio H.D. found that reading in Helen's voice energized her, imbuing her 'with a self-assurance that I generally lack in every-day life'.[27] The prose introductions she wrote for these sessions inspired her to write prose interludes or captions for every poem in the volume, prose that serves as summary, clarification and, often, counterpoint to the verse – creating a dialectic between prose and verse that serves to heighten the poem's destabilizing 'conclusions'. The poem is an epic that redefines the epic.

From 1946 to 1953, H.D. lived alone in Switzerland. She and Bryher had often arranged their travel plans such that she had several months alone to write each year, but she had never experienced such solitude. She saw Bryher frequently and hosted other visitors: Perdita and her family, Bryher's childhood friend Doris Long, psychoanalysts Walter and Melitta Schmideberg, Kenneth Macpherson and his partner Islay de Lyon, Norman Douglas, Robert Herring, Silvia Dobson, Faith Mackenzie and H.D.'s astrologer Elizabeth Ashby. In most years, she and Bryher continued the tradition of celebrating their September birthdays together, and

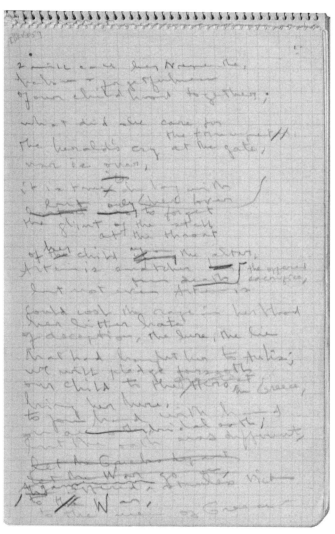

Helen in Egypt, 'Pallinode', notebook draft, 1950s.

they took occasional trips together to Italy and to the United States. Though H.D. does complain at times that she misses Bryher and feels she doesn't see enough of her, she was for the most part content to spend her time reading and writing.

In early 1953, however, H.D. had an operation for an abdominal intestinal occlusion in Lausanne. The recovery was not uncomplicated, and she re-entered the hospital several months later, following a hurried trip to the United States to meet her second grandchild, Nicholas. When she was finally well enough to leave the Clinique Cécil, she returned to Klinik Brunner to convalesce. A new pattern was established, as she migrated back and forth between Zurich and Lugano, putting more distance between herself and Bryher, who was busy jet-setting around the world when she wasn't at home at Kenwin. The two continued to correspond regularly whenever apart, and they talked by phone once a week.

Initially a reluctant denizen of Klinik Brunner, H.D. was surprised to find how much she ultimately came to embrace its social life. She revelled in the conversation and the gossip, enjoying the communal dinners at the end of each day. In a memoir of the period, she imagined, 'I dream of a sort of retreat, *Magic Mountain* where they could come and stay, rest, have proper food, books, all the attractions of our buzzing little metropolis, specialists, at beck and call.'[28] At Brunner, in July of 1953 – just before she began the second part of *Helen in Egypt* – H.D. met Erich Heydt, a young bisexual (and probably bipolar) doctor who had trained in existential psychotherapy. This meeting would prove to be momentous, for Erich would become her doctor, her co-analyst, her friend and her confessor. Unlike Freud – who both admired and pathologized creativity – Erich understood and respected the unique needs of an artist. H.D. and Erich shared notes and planned strategies for the multinational group of patients flowing in and out of the sanatorium. At last, she could put her training as lay analyst to use. As Heydt explained,

With H.D.'s deep interest in the mind's working, her
knowledge of psychodynamics, her love for unusual,
eccentric, even strange personalities, she was fascinated by
the problems (psychiatric and otherwise) of the guests, and
she took a lively interest in the Sanatorium community.
She was sought out regularly by patients as a 'wise lady',
as a confidante, and as an auxiliary therapist.[29]

Among her 'patients' were Joan Waluga, the troubled daughter of
Bryher's schoolfriend Doris Long, and Walter Schmideberg, who
had once been her analyst but who died at the Klinik Brunner of
complications related to his alcoholism. (His death in 1954 ignited
tension with Bryher for a time, as H.D.'s anger was sparked at
discovering how close he and Bryher had been.[30])

H.D.'s spirited life at Küsnacht is recorded in her journal-
style memoir, *Compassionate Friendship* (penned in 1955), and
her last novel, *Magic Mirror* (written in 1956), which fictionalizes
observations recorded in its companion memoir. While the novel
surveys her relationship with Heydt and the therapeutic work she
does with the Klinik inhabitants, it is also a study of memory, and
the recovery of memory. This final novel is about how narrative
governs memory, and about how our perceptions shift as we age.
Magic Mirror, too, is about the writer's role in recording these
stories. In keeping with *Helen*'s resistance to finality, she later
declared, '*Majic Mirror* is not finished, actually it is a book that
never could be finished.'[31] Like all of her 1950s and '60s writings,
it maintains a focus on process, not product.

H.D. turned seventy in 1956, celebrating with a trip to the United
States. There she spent time with her third grandchild, Elizabeth
Bryher, attended a special birthday exhibition Pearson organized
for her at Yale and played tour guide to Pearson and Bryher on a
trip to her home town of Bethlehem. But her life would change
irrevocably weeks after she returned to Küsnacht. On 5 November

1956, she slipped on a throw rug and broke her hip. She was treated at the Hirslanden Klinik, but she would never fully recover her ability to walk without 'sticks', as she called her crutches. There would be no end to that suffering, only an unending process of healing. This accident impaired her mobility such that it put an end to her migratory lifestyle. She was forced to live at Klinik Brunner year-round.

Treatment entailed lengthy periods of bed rest in which she was 'forced to live in the trying, humiliating outer minutiae of life'.[32] During her protracted convalescence, she began a dream journal, *Hirslanden Notebooks*, that offers a sense of her everyday existence, even as it presents a retrospective of her life, her spiritual quest and her corpus. In between exhausting physical therapy sessions, she jotted down her experience of depression stemming from her deprivation, her memories of the past and her interpretations of her dreams. *Compassionate Friendship* and her *Hirslanden Notebooks* continued a project of such ruminations on her life and work begun in 1949 with her essay 'H.D. by Delia Alton' (1949–50), and completed a year before her death in another memoir, *Thorn Thicket* (1960). Her accident and its aftermath were not ultimately an obstacle to her work; quite the opposite, she could make use of the experience. As poet Robert Duncan observed of H.D.'s aesthetic, 'H.D. will all her life be concerned in her work with conveying to our sympathy the fact that agony seems to be in the very nature of deep experience, that in every instant there is a painful – painful in its intensity – revelation.'[33] Perdita remembered with admiration, H.D. took it all in stride, as best she could, 'swinging her crutches, making them part of her act', moving awkwardly but vigorously, 'infinitely calmer, witty, thoroughly delightful'.[34]

There was still much more writing to come. Another memoir, *End to Torment*, was written in 1958 at Pearson's invitation. In this work, reflections on her past intrude persistently on the present day, as H.D. avers that 'the laurel wreath of the acclaimed

H.D., 1950.

achievement must be tempered, balanced, re-lived, re-focused or even sustained by the unpredictable, the inchoate'.[35] It is in part a meditation on Ezra Pound – an article in *The Nation* about his confinement at St Elizabeth's served as catalyst for the book. Fond memories of their youthful companionship stand in an unresolved, and unresolvable, dialectic with her troubling knowledge of the older Pound, who had delivered pro-Fascist radio addresses during the Second World War and who continued to spout antisemitic hate speech well after war's end. But the book is also a meditation, by an ageing writer, on the nature of memory as unstable and unreliable. It theorizes the extent to which a memory is pure construction, admitting near the end that her memories of Pound may well be fictions. In that sense, she uses the occasion of the memoir to continue her analysis of how narrative and amnesia function politically and to problematize the very genre in which she was writing.

In her more sympathetic moments during the war, she had wondered if Pound's rantings were just evidence of mental illness.[36] But she was not, ultimately, so charitable. If Pearson was expecting something laudatory, he may have been disappointed, but having lived through the war, and having had dear friends incarcerated in a concentration camp, H.D. was not going to deliver an unqualified encomium. Likewise, she refused to sign a petition, organized by the poet Robert Frost, demanding Pound's release from St Elizabeth's. Her anger, too, extended to Dorothy, his wife, who had defended a revisionist account of the Blitz.[37] She felt closer to Pound's long-time extramarital partner, the violinist Olga Rudge.

In the years before H.D. died, she was still writing poetry, too. As a whole, *Vale Ave* (1957), *Sagesse* (1957–8), *Winter Love* (1959) and *Hermetic Definition* (1960–61) strike the same postmodern chord that *Helen in Egypt* does. H.D. was no longer using art to stitch together some sense of unity or harmony but rather to explore the process of the quest for truth. Like *Helen in Egypt*, these late poems utilize a dialectical structure, employing polyvocality to complicate synthesis. In *Winter Love*, a strophe and antistrophe debate whether fate is heavy or hung on a delicate thread, and whether or not art can have an impact on culture. Voices clash and intrude upon one another. The speaker asserts, then retracts. As Duncan put it to poet Denise Levertov, 'she disturbs the poem's (the poet's) voice with her own'.[38] The past and the present coexist with no promise of resolution.

These late poems bear images and ideas derived from her research into Ambelain's Kabbalism, that system that, for her, integrated the disparate shards of her always evolving spiritual sense. H.D.'s misreading of 'astral poet' for 'actual poet' in a letter from Robert Duncan delighted her, and we might well regard these poems as compositions of the 'astral H.D.'[39] The themes are familiar ones: women's sexuality, the poet-soldier or 'héros fatale', the pernicious 'romantic thralldom' of heterosexual love, and the imbrication of the personal in the political.[40] In her old age, H.D. isn't seducing male devotees but imagining them as archetypes: in *Vale Ave*, for instance, Lord Hugh Dowding, the RAF officer whose forays into spiritualism inspired H.D.'s own investigations, is doubled, by Kabbalistic logic, with Julius Caesar, the Renaissance explorer and courtier Sir Walter Raleigh, the biblical Adam and the fallen angel Lucifer. While a number of men serve as objects of desire

Ezra Pound, 1950s.

in these poems, they are somewhat interchangeable figures who arouse, incite and inspire the woman poet, even as they objectify her and fail to appreciate or honour her work and her autonomy. If her many 1920s novels plumb the trauma of being married to Aldington, a poet-soldier, these poems portray men she is not involved with romantically and, in several cases, she barely knows, or doesn't know at all. The lover is at once 'new to me, different', but 'of an old, old sphere' just the same.[41] 'The torch was lit from another before you,' the speaker intones in *Hermetic Definition*, 'and another and another before that,' as she conflates three Black men she admired (and lusted after): the journalist Lionel Durand, Paul Robeson and Rafer Johnson, a U.S. decathlon star.[42] The woman artist figure – in *Vale Ave*, Raleigh's imagined lover Elizabeth Dyer, Caesar's paramour Julia, the biblical Lilith and H.D. herself – is tasked with recovering cultural memory to break this cycle.

This degree of abstraction both reifies the link between sex and art that H.D. found so generative as early as the 1910s and criticizes her reliance on men and the wars they wage for poetic inspiration. She is writing a critique of love poetry in the genre of the love poem. To be sure, these late poems can be racier than her previous verse, as she expresses a vibrant female sexuality undeterred by her advanced years. 'I am really <u>out</u> of myself, scribbling a sort of "popular" love sequence, through the ages – I am sure Pearson would be shocked,' H.D. confessed gleefully to Aldington in the midst of writing *Vale Ave*.[43] The ever-present image of the rose is imbued with mystical significance in these poems, but it is also representative of female genitalia. 'Few can endure/ the ecstasy, the fever/ the folding and unfolding of a flower', she writes in *Sagesse*, a poem that takes Heydt as its muse.[44] Her final poem, *Hermetic Definition*, is addressed to the Haitian *Newsweek* interviewer Lionel Durand, who travelled to Switzerland to interview her in 1960 when *Bid Me to Live* appeared. It is Durand, in part, who inspired the recurrent refrain, 'the reddest rose unfolds':

Why did you come
to trouble my decline?
I am old (I was old till you came);

the reddest rose unfolds,
(which is ridiculous
in this time, this place,

unseemly, impossible,
even slightly scandalous),
the reddest rose unfolds[45]

Winter Love reimagines her early romance with Pound, as H.D.
returns to Helen for one last poem, casting Ezra as Odysseus.

In *Helen in Egypt* and *Winter Love*, 'desire and sexuality are
destructive and empowering at the same time.'[46] Lurking beneath
passion is judgement; after all, Durand had called her novel *Bid
Me to Live* 'precious'.[47] The woman poet is never deemed equal to
the man. The deific Lady bids her, 'write, write or die', but how to
extricate her art from the 'bondage' of the 'rose so red'?[48] 'I did not
realize that separation/ was the only solution.'[49] The poem gives
birth to the lover, but, she demands, 'Now you are born/ and it's all
over,/ will you leave me alone?'[50]

These poems reveal H.D.'s vexation over her lack of mobility
as well. Of *Vale Ave*, the first poem written after H.D. broke her
hip, Cynthia Hogue notes how this frustration registers even at
the level of form: 'The incantatory rhythms and sonic resonance
have not disappeared, but are juxtaposed with moments of
hesitance, anxious self-reflection lodging fragments of memories,
and a discursive hybridity.'[51] *Sagesse* is grounded in the quotidian,
'rupturing lyric with everyday discursiveness'.[52] The speaker is
plagued with constant insomnia, and she summons angels to keep
her company in the early morning hours. The poem exposes the

horrors of the material world – the infirmities of old age, but also the terrors of war – and the ultimate failure of taking solace from the spiritual realm.

As H.D. aged, her star was on the rise. On Pearson's advice, H.D. repatriated as a U.S. citizen in 1958, and her final years were filled with American poetry awards, including the Harriet Monroe Memorial Prize, the Brandeis University Creative Arts Award for Poetry, the Longview Award and a Distinguished Service citation from Bryn Mawr. The most prestigious award was from the American Academy of Arts and Letters. On 25 May 1960, H.D. became the first woman to receive the Award of Merit Medal for Poetry, a prize she claimed amidst raucous applause, and while it was 'definitely not her scene', she nonetheless basked in the attention.[53] When in New York to accept the award, she submitted to a rare interview with the press, for the *New York Herald Tribune*. Having fled the States in 1911 to pursue her craft in Europe, where the arts were valued, she told the interviewer, Harriet Stix, that she was now convinced that 'America has changed. Europe has changed . . . The arts are more vital here now than in Europe.'[54] On this trip, she was also able to greet her fourth (and last) grandchild, Timothy. (Had he been a girl, she would have been named Hilda.)

With these accolades came the adoration of a new generation of poets, Robert Duncan and Denise Levertov among them. Both poets met and corresponded with her, and H.D. bestowed tempered but warm appreciation on their verse. Identifying with her queerness, her aesthetics and her idiosyncratic spirituality, Duncan wrote poems in dialogue with hers, and his near seven-hundred-page prose volume *The H.D. Book* is an incredible testament to her influence on him and his peers: 'For my own generation, our elders – for me, specifically Pound, H.D., [William Carlos] Williams, and [D. H.] Lawrence – remain primary generative forces.'[55] He had discovered her *Trilogy* in the late 1940s and followed her career until her death: 'In smoky rooms in Berkeley, in painters' studios

'Hermetic Definition', notebook draft, 1960.

in San Francisco, I read these works aloud; dreamed about them; took my life in them; studied them as my anatomy of what Poetry must be.'[56] Today, poets as diverse as Nathaniel Mackey, Susan Howe and Carolyn Forché cite H.D.'s poetry as important to their own development as artists. In fact, for all of her reading of and writing about history, H.D. kept abreast of contemporary literature. She was awed by W. H. Auden, and she grew to like the work of

H.D., 1950s.

Faulkner and Hemingway in her later years. Though she professed that she did not much like 'angry young men', she was nonetheless a fan of the beat poets. 'I feel they are looking for something,' she told Durand.[57]

Even in her final decade, H.D. retained a youthful air. As late as 1959 she petitioned Bryher (unsuccessfully) to be permitted driving lessons.[58] Durand's account of his interview depicted her as an energetic writer whose mind was 'still aflame with provocative thoughts, strong opinions, and the literary temper'.[59] Heydt, too, described her as 'most youthful, enthusiastic, open to everything new – not at all "old".' She never complained, ever, he insisted.[60] He was, in fact, convinced that her reluctance to complain about heart pain – pain that hadn't deterred her from completing final corrections for *Hermetic Definition* – delayed her treatment until too late to prevent her stroke in June of 1961. There was undoubtedly another factor as well. Just two months earlier, she had been abruptly uprooted from her home at the Klinik Brunner, after Brunner's son decided to sell the facility, and she had suffered a difficult transition to the Hotel Sonnenberg, where she was much more isolated. In her *Hirslanden Notebooks*, she recalled the 'curious, broken sometimes nightmarish nights' following the move, even as she reassured friends and family that she was content there.[61]

H.D.'s final diary entry of 2 June 1961 – about a woman who did not speak – feels eerily prescient when one considers what happened just a few weeks later. The stroke interfered irrevocably with her ability to communicate, a terrible fate for a writer. Both Duncan and Levertov were troubled by the terrible irony when Pearson explained, 'The part of the brain which controls speech has been injured . . . Yet she does have fiercely the desire to communicate, and strikes her breast in passionate frustration when there is no word at her tongue's tip.'[62] 'They are not dying,' Levertov wrote of H.D. and her cohort:

they are withdrawn
into a painful privacy

learning to live without words.
E. P. 'It looks like dying' – Williams: 'I can't
describe to you what has been

happening to me' –
H. D. 'unable to speak'.[63]

Levertov's generation of versifiers is left to 'count the/ words in our pockets', and 'wonder how it will be without them'. 'The flame has fled/ making but words of what I loved', Duncan wrote in 'Doves', his poem about H.D.'s aphasia.[64] Duncan knew her well; 'if she has lost words in waking life,' he fretted, 'she will have lost them in dreams too.'[65]

H.D. never recovered. Bryher and Perdita, who had rushed over from the States, tended to her as they squabbled over whether she should remain in Switzerland or be moved to a home in the United States, near her daughter. But H.D. lived just three months after the stroke. She died on 27 September 1961, shortly after Bryher showed her the final proofs of *Helen in Egypt*. She was cremated, and her ashes were laid at Nisky Hill Cemetery in Bethlehem, Pennsylvania, in the Doolittle family plot. Her gravestone bears an inscription taken from her poem 'Epitaph':

Greek flower; Greek ecstasy
reclaims for ever
one who died
following
intricate song's lost measure.[66]

References

Introduction

1   H.D., *Collected Poems, 1912–1944*, ed. Louis L. Martz (New York, 1983), p. 21.
2   Ibid., pp. 14, 5, 19.
3   H.D., *Trilogy*, ed. Aliki Barnstone (New York, 1998), p. 59.
4   H.D., *Collected Poems*, p. 300.
5   Sarah Parker and Jade French, '"But with this I'm embodied": H.D.'s Public Photographic Portraits, 1913–1956', *Feminist Modernist Studies*, IV/1 (2021), pp. 93–124 (p. 93).
6   H.D., 'Narthex', in *The Second American Caravan*, ed. Alfred Kreymborg, Lewis Mumford and Paul Rosenfeld (New York, 1928), p. 281.
7   Robert Duncan, *The H.D. Book*, ed. Michael Boughn and Victor Coleman (Berkeley, CA, 2011), p. 242.
8   Letter from Silvia Dobson to Bryher dated 6 March 1966. Bryher Papers, General Collection, Beinecke Rare Book and Manuscript Library, Yale University, New Haven, Connecticut.
9   Ann Laura Stoler, 'Colonial Archives and the Arts of Governance', *Archival Science*, II/1–2 (2002), pp. 87–109 (p. 90).
10 Diane Wood Middlebrook, 'Postmodernism and the Biographer', in *Revealing Lives: Autobiography, Biography, and Gender*, ed. Susan Groag Bell and Marilyn Yalom (Albany, NY, 1990), pp. 155–66 (p. 156).
11 Llewellin Jegels, 'Both Sides Now: Reflections on Writing Zayn Adam's Biography', *a/b: Auto/Biography Studies*, XXXVI/2 (2021), pp. 291–302 (pp. 292–3).
12 H.D., *Paint It Today*, ed. Cassandra Laity (New York, 1992), p. 27.
13 H. P. Collins, 'H.D.', Norman Holmes Pearson Papers, Yale Collection of American Literature, Beinecke Rare Book and Manuscript Library, New Haven, Connecticut.

14 Frances Gregg, *The Mystic Leeway*, ed. Ben Jones (Ottawa, ON, 1995), p. 70.

15 James Whitall, *English Years* (San Diego, CA, 1935), p. 55.

16 Ibid., p. 65.

17 H.D., 'Narthex', in *The Second American Caravan*, ed. Alfred Kreymborg, Lewis Mumford and Paul Rosenfeld (New York, 1928), pp. 240, 271.

18 H.D., *Paint It Today*, pp. 25, 24.

19 H.D., *Bid Me to Live (A Madrigal)*, ed. Caroline Zilboorg (Gainesville, FL, 2014), p. 181.

20 H.D., *White Rose and the Red*, ed. Alison Halsall (Gainesville, FL, 2009), p. 238.

21 Middlebrook, 'Postmodernism', p. 159.

22 Perdita Schaffner, 'Sketch of H.D.: The Egyptian Cat', in H.D., *Hedylus* (Redding Ridge, CT, 1980), p. 145.

1 'inexorably entangled', 1886–1911

1 H.D., *HERmione* (New York, 1981), p. 203.

2 Ibid., p. 4.

3 Ibid., p. 8.

4 Ibid., p. 192.

5 H.D., *Tribute to Freud* (New York, 1984), p. 28.

6 Ibid., p. 31; R. H. Tucker, 'Charles Leander Doolittle', *Publications of the Astronomical Society of the Pacific*, XXXI/108 (1919), p. 104.

7 H.D., *Hirslanden Notebooks*, ed. Matte Robinson and Demetres P. Tryphonopoulos (Victoria, BC, 2012), p. 9.

8 H.D., *Tribute to Freud*, p. 19.

9 Ibid., p. 24.

10 H.D., *Majic Ring*, ed. Demetres P. Tryphonopoulos (Gainesville, FL, 2009), p. 94.

11 H.D., *Tribute to Freud*, pp. 20, 21.

12 Francis Wolle, *A Moravian Heritage* (Boulder, CO, 1972), p. 20.

13 Silvia Dobson Papers, Beinecke Rare Book and Manuscript Library, Yale University, New Haven, Connecticut.

14 H.D., *Tribute to Freud*, p. 186.

15 Ibid., p. 185.
16 Susan Stanford Friedman, 'Remembering Shakespeare Always, but Remembering Him Differently', *Sagetrieb*, II/2 (1983), p. 59 n. 27.
17 Letter from H.D. to Viola Baxter Jordan dated 30 August [1942]. Viola Baxter Jordan Papers, Beinecke Rare Book and Manuscript Library, Yale University, New Haven, Connecticut.
18 H.D., *Tribute to Freud*, p. 132.
19 On H.D.'s education, see Emily Mitchell Wallace, 'Athene's Owl', *Poesis*, VI/3–4 (1985), pp. 98–123.
20 H.D., 'From H.D.', in *The Cantos of Ezra Pound: Some Testimonies* (New York, 1933), p. 17.
21 A. David Moody, *Ezra Pound*, vol. I: *The Young Genius, 1885–1920* (New York, 2010), pp. 15, 19.
22 H.D., *Paint It Today*, ed. Cassandra Laity (New York, 1992), p. 7.
23 H.D., *End to Torment* (New York, 1979), p. 3.
24 John Gould Fletcher, *Life Is My Song* (New York, 1937), p. 59.
25 H.D., 'From H.D.', p. 17; H.D., *End to Torment*, p. 4.
26 H.D., *End to Torment*, 38.
27 Helen Carr, *The Verse Revolutionaries: Ezra Pound, H.D. and the Imagists* (London, 2013), p. 53.
28 William Carlos Williams, *The Selected Letters of William Carlos Williams*, ed. John C. Thirwall (New York, 1984), p. 9.
29 Letter from H.D. to William Carlos Williams dated 26 March 1908, in David A. Rice, ed., '"Dear Billy": H.D.'s Letters to William Carlos Williams', *William Carlos Williams Review*, XXIII/2 (1997), pp. 27–34 (p. 43).
30 Letter from H.D. to William Carlos Williams dated 23 January 1907, in Rice, ed., '"Dear Billy"', p. 35.
31 Oliver Marlow Wilkinson, 'Frances Gregg: First Hand', in Frances Gregg, *The Mystic Leeway*, ed. Ben Jones (Ottawa, ON, 1995), p. 21.
32 H.D., *HERmione*, p. 52.
33 H.D., *Paint It Today*, pp. 7, 9.
34 H.D., *End to Torment*, p. 3.
35 Cassandra Laity, 'H.D. and A. C. Swinburne: Decadence and Modernist Women's Writing', *Feminist Studies*, XV/3 (1989), pp. 461–84 (p. 471).
36 H.D., *Paint It Today*, p. 22.
37 Gregg, *The Mystic Leeway*, p. 94.

38 H.D., *Paint It Today*, p. 10.
39 Gregg, *The Mystic Leeway*, p. 93.
40 Ibid., p. 70.
41 Ben Jones, 'Editor's Introduction', in Gregg, *The Mystic Leeway*, p. 4.
42 Gregg, *The Mystic Leeway*, p. 69.
43 Ibid., p. 65.
44 H.D., *HERmione*, pp. 143, 149.
45 H.D. Papers, Yale Collection of American Literature, Beinecke Rare Book and Manuscript Library, New Haven, Connecticut.
46 Letter from H.D. to Norman Holmes Pearson dated 5 September [1949], in *Between History and Poetry: The Letters of H.D. and Norman Holmes Pearson*, ed. Donna Krolik Hollenberg (Iowa City, IA, 1997), p. 91.
47 H.D., autobiographical notes. H.D. Papers.
48 H.D., *HERmione*, p. 80.

2 'my pencil run riot!', 1911–14

1 F. T. Marinetti, 'The Founding and Manifesto of Futurism' [1909], in *Futurism: An Anthology*, ed. Christine Poggi, Lawrence Rainey and Laura Wittman (New Haven, CT, 2009), p. 51.
2 F. T. Marinetti, 'We Abjure Our Symbolist Masters' [1911], in *Futurism: An Anthology*, ed. Poggi, Rainey and Wittman, p. 94.
3 Margaret Anderson, ed., 'Confessions-Questionnaire', *The Little Review Anthology* (New York, 1970), p. 365.
4 H.D., *Tribute to Freud* (New York, 1984), p. 153.
5 Frances Gregg, *The Mystic Leeway*, ed. Ben Jones (Ottawa, ON, 1995), p. 107.
6 Ibid., p. 151; H.D. Papers, Yale Collection of American Literature, Beinecke Rare Book and Manuscript Library, New Haven, Connecticut.
7 Gregg, *The Mystic Leeway*, p. 109.
8 Ibid., p. 108.
9 Frances Gregg, 'Hermaphroditus', *Others*, I/4 (1915), p. 77.
10 H.D., *Asphodel*, ed. Robert Spoo (Durham, NC, 1992), p. 53.
11 Ibid., p. 4.
12 Ibid., pp. 9–10, 13.

13 Gregg, *The Mystic Leeway*, pp. 121, 119.

14 Ibid., p. 120.

15 H.D., *Asphodel*, pp. 38–9.

16 Gregg, *The Mystic Leeway*, p. 131.

17 Walter Morse Rummel, *Ten Songs for Children Young and Old* (London, 1914). On H.D.'s contributions, see Chris Brown, 'H.D. and Rummel's *Songs for Children*: A Lyrical Collaboration', *H.D. Newsletter*, II/1 (1988), pp. 4–11.

18 H.D., *Paint It Today*, ed. Cassandra Laity (New York, 1992), p. 25.

19 Gregg, *The Mystic Leeway*, p. 146.

20 Louis U. Wilkinson, *The Buffoon* (New York, 1916), p. 108.

21 H.D., *Asphodel*, pp. 52–3.

22 Gemma Bristow, 'Brief Encounter: Richard Aldington and the Englishwoman', *English Literature in Transition, 1880–1920*, XLIX/1 (2006), pp. 3–13 (p. 8).

23 Postcard from H.D. to Helen Wolle Doolittle dated 17 November 1911. H.D. Papers.

24 H.D., 'The Suffragette', ed. Donna Krolik Hollenberg, *Sagetrieb*, XV/1 and 2 (1996), pp. 5–7.

25 Brigit Patmore, *This Impassioned Onlooker* (London, 1926), p. v.

26 Susan Stanford Friedman and Rachel Blau DuPlessis, '"I had two loves separate": The Sexualities of H.D.'s *HER*', in *Signets: Reading H.D.*, ed. Stanford Friedman and Blau DuPlessis (Madison, WI, 1990), pp. 205–32 (p. 228 n.5).

27 H.D., diary. H.D. Papers.

28 Richard Aldington, *Life for Life's Sake: A Book of Reminiscences* (London, 1941), pp. 111–12.

29 Vivien Whelpton, *Richard Aldington: Poet, Soldier, Lover, 1911–1929* (Cambridge, 2019), p. 52.

30 Aldington, *Life for Life's Sake*, pp. 62–3.

31 Charles Doyle, *Richard Aldington* (Carbondale, IL, 1989), pp. 10–11.

32 Whelpton, *Richard Aldington*, p. 33.

33 John Gould Fletcher, *Life Is My Song* (New York, 1937), pp. 78–9.

34 James Whitall, *English Years* (San Diego, CA, 1935), p. 55.

35 H.D., *Paint It Today*, p. 37.

36 H.D., *Asphodel*, p. 134.

37 Aldington, *Life for Life's Sake*, p. 138.

38 Letter from Richard Aldington to H.D. dated 20 March 1929, in *Richard Aldington and H.D.: Their Lives in Letters*, ed. Caroline Zilboorg (Manchester, 2003), p. 192.

39 Cyrena N. Pondrom, 'H.D. and the Origins of Imagism', *Sagetrieb*, IV/1 (1985), p. 99.

40 Aldington, *Life for Life's Sake*, p. 133.

41 Ibid., p. 134.

42 Harriet Monroe, 'The Open Door', *Poetry*, I/2 (1912), p. 64.

43 H.D., *Collected Poems*, pp. 37–9.

44 Whelpton, *Richard Aldington*, p. 64.

45 H.D., diary. H.D. Papers.

46 H.D., *Paint It Today*, p. 44.

47 Whelpton, *Richard Aldington*, p. 70.

48 Diana Collecott, *H.D. and Sapphic Modernism: 1910–1950* (New York, 1999), p. 66.

49 Gregg, *The Mystic Leeway*, p. 15.

50 Frances Gregg, 'To H.D.', *Poetry*, V/4 (1915), p. 166; H.D., *Collected Poems*, p. 29.

51 On Marsden and Pound, see Bruce Clarke, 'Dora Marsden and Ezra Pound: "The New Freewoman" and "The Serious Artist"', *Contemporary Literature*, XXXIII/1 (1992), pp. 91–112.

52 Rebecca West, 'Imagisme', *New Freewoman*, V/1 (1913), pp. 86–7.

53 Annette Debo, *The American H.D.* (Iowa City, IA, 2011), p. 134.

54 Lesley Wheeler, 'Mapping Sea Garden', in *Approaches to Teaching H.D.'s Poetry and Prose*, ed. Annette Debo and Lara Vetter (New York, 2011), p. 40.

55 H.D., *Collected Poems*, pp. 5, 14.

56 Ibid., pp. 26, 20.

57 Ibid., p. 21.

58 Ibid., p. 20.

59 John Gould Fletcher, 'H.D.'s Vision', *Poetry*, IX/5 (1917), p. 267.

60 H.D., *Collected Poems*, p. 8.

61 Ibid., p. 36.

62 Ibid., pp. 22, 28.

63 Amy Lowell, *Tendencies in Modern American Poetry* (New York, 1917), p. 257.

64 H.D., *Collected Poems*, pp. 40, 41.

65 Review of H.D., *Sea Garden*, *Times Literary Supplement* (5 October 1916), p. 479.
66 Lowell, *Tendencies*, p. 245.

3 'the black cloud fell', 1914–18

1 H.D., *Tribute to Freud* (New York, 1984), p. 150.
2 Richard Aldington, *Life for Life's Sake: A Book of Reminiscences* (London, 1941), pp. 161, 171.
3 John Gould Fletcher, *Life Is My Song* (New York, 1937), p. 177.
4 Louis Silverstein, 'H.D. Chronology, Part Two', available at www. imagists.org, accessed 28 July 2022.
5 Letter from H.D. to Amy Lowell dated 23 November 1914. Amy Lowell correspondence, MS Lowell 19–19.4, MS Lowell 19, (8), Box: 1, Houghton Library, Boston, Massachusetts.
6 Letter from H.D. to F. S. Flint dated [5(?) July 1915], in H.D., 'Selected Letters from H.D. to F. S. Flint: A Commentary on the Imagist Period', *Contemporary Literature*, X/4 (1969), p. 563.
7 Letter from H.D. to Amy Lowell dated 17 December 1914. Amy Lowell correspondence.
8 Richard Aldington, 'Modern Poetry and the Imagists', *The Egoist*, II/1 (1914), p. 202.
9 See Gillian Hanscombe and Virginia L. Smyers, *Writing for Their Lives: The Modernist Women, 1910–1940* (London, 1987), pp. 199–202.
10 Paul Bradley Bellew, '"At the Mercy of Editorial Selection": Amy Lowell, Ezra Pound, and the Imagist Anthologies', *Journal of Modern Literature*, XL/2 (2017), pp. 22–40 (p. 24).
11 Aldington, *Life for Life's Sake*, p. 135.
12 Conrad Aiken, 'The Place of Imagism', *New Republic* (22 May 1915), pp. 75–6.
13 William Stanley Braithwaite, 'Imagism: Another View', *New Republic* (12 June 1915), pp. 154–5.
14 Letter from H.D. to Norman Holmes Pearson dated 13 March [1957]. Norman Holmes Pearson Papers, Yale Collection of American Literature, Beinecke Rare Book and Manuscript Library, New Haven, Connecticut.
15 'Manifesto-I' and 'Manifesto-II', *BLAST*, 1 (1914), pp. 11, 39.

16 Ezra Pound, 'Vortex', *BLAST*, 1 (1914), p. 154.

17 Fletcher, *Life Is My Song*, p. 151.

18 Letter from Richard Aldington to Amy Lowell dated 21 May 1915, in Hanscome and Smyers, *Writing for Their Lives*, p. 28.

19 H.D., *Asphodel*, ed. Robert Spoo (Durham, NC, 1992), p. 115.

20 H.D., *Bid Me to Live (A Madrigal)*, ed. Caroline Zilboorg (Gainesville, FL, 2014), p. 18.

21 H. P. Collins, 'H.D.' Norman Holmes Pearson Papers.

22 Richard Aldington, *Richard Aldington: An Autobiography in Letters*, ed. Norman T. Gates (University Park, PA, 1992), p. 18.

23 On H.D.'s role in the series, see Caroline Zilboorg, 'Joint Venture: Richard Aldington, H.D. and the Poets' Translation Series', *Philological Quarterly*, LXX/1 (1991), pp. 67–98.

24 Ibid., p. 70; Elizabeth Vandiver, '"Seeking . . . buried beauty": The Poet's Translation Series', in *The Classics in Modernist Translation*, ed. Miranda Hickman and Lynn Kozak (New York, 2019), p. 8.

25 Zilboorg, 'Joint Venture', p. 74.

26 H.D., 'Notes on Euripides, Pausanius, and Greek Lyrice Poets', H.D. Papers, Yale Collection of American Literature, Beinecke Rare Book and Manuscript Library, New Haven, Connecticut.

27 Helen Carr, *The Verse Revolutionaries: Ezra Pound, H.D. and the Imagists* (London, 2013), p. 56; Susan McCabe, *H.D. and Bryher: An Untold Love Story of Modernism* (New York, 2021), p. 43.

28 Eileen Gregory, *H.D. and Hellenism: Classic Lines* (New York, 1997), p. 124.

29 H.D., *Choruses from the Iphigeneia in Aulis and the Hippolytus of Euripides* (London, 1919), p. 6.

30 Ibid., p. 11.

31 Ibid., pp. 13–14.

32 Ibid., pp. 16–17.

33 Ibid., p. 21.

34 [J. W. McKail], 'A Note of the Classic Revival', *Times Literary Supplement* (4 May 1916), p. 210.

35 T. S. Eliot, 'Review of *The Poets' Translation Series*', *Poetry*, IX/2 (1916), pp. 102–3.

36 T. S. Eliot, *The Letters of T. S. Eliot*, vol. I: *1898–1922* (New York, 1988), p. 200.

37 Donna Krolik Hollenberg, *Winged Words: The Life and Work of the Poet H.D.* (Ann Arbor, MI, 2022), p. 61.

38 H.D., *Collected Poems, 1912–1944*, ed. Louis L. Martz (New York, 1983), pp. 310–15.

39 Letter from Richard Aldington to John Cournos dated 2 November 1916, in *The Dearest Friend: A Selection from the Letters of Richard Aldington to John Cournos*, ed. R. T. Risk (Francestown, NH, 1978), p. 12.

40 Letter from Richard Aldington to F. S. Flint dated 12 November 1916, in *Imagist Dialogues*, ed. Michael Copp (Cambridge, 2009), p. 151.

41 Letter from Richard Aldington to F. S. Flint dated [22 November 1916], in *Imagist Dialogues*, p. 155.

42 Fletcher, *Life Is My Song*, p. 243.

43 H.D., 'Marianne Moore', *The Egoist*, III/8 (1916), p. 119.

44 Letter from Richard Aldington to F. S. Flint dated 22 January 1917, in *Imagist Dialogues*, p. 173.

45 John Cournos, *Autobiography* (New York, 1935), p. 269.

46 Letter from H.D. to John Cournos dated 8[?] September 1916, in 'Art and Ardor in World War One: Selected Letters from H.D. to John Cournos', ed. Donna Krolik Hollenberg, *Iowa Review*, XVI/3 (1986), pp. 126–55 (p. 134).

47 Letter from H.D. to John Cournos dated 13 September 1916, ibid., p. 135.

48 Alfred Satterthwaite, 'John Cournos and "H.D."', *Twentieth Century Literature*, XXII/4 (1976), pp. 394–410 (p. 410).

49 Ibid., p. 403.

50 H.D., *Bid Me to Live*, p. 8.

51 Fletcher, *Life Is My Song*, p. 231.

52 Ibid., 244.

53 Brigit Patmore, 'Conversations with Lawrence', *London Magazine*, IV/6 (1957), p. 34.

54 'Confessions-Questionnaire', in *The Little Review Anthology*, ed. Margaret Anderson (New York, 1970), p. 365.

55 H.D., *Bid Me to Live*, p. 51.

56 Ibid., p. 62.

57 Ibid., pp. 86, 128.

58 H.D., *Tribute to Freud*, p. 134.

59 H.D., *Asphodel*, pp. 143, 148.

60 Vivien Whelpton, *Richard Aldington: Poet, Soldier, Lover, 1911–1929* (Cambridge, 2019), p. 164.

61   H.D., *Tribute to Freud*, pp. 145, 186.
62   H.D., *Bid Me to Live*, pp. 162, 163.
63   Letter from Richard Aldington to H.D. dated 20 May 1918, in *Richard Aldington: An Autobiography in Letters*, p. 33.
64   Letter from Richard Aldington to F. S. Flint dated 2 June 1918, in *Imagist Dialogues*, p. 220.
65   Letter from Richard Aldington to H.D. dated 7 July 1918, in *Richard Aldington: An Autobiography in Letters*, p. 83.
66   H.D., *Magic Mirror, Compassionate Friendship, Thorn Thicket*, ed. Nephie J. Christodoulides (Victoria, BC, 2012), p. 170.
67   Richard Aldington, *Death of a Hero* (London, 1984), p. 323.
68   Ibid., p. 226.
69   Ibid., pp. 228, 372.
70   H.D., *Bid Me to Live*, p. 8; H.D., *Paint It Today*, p. 63.
71   H.D., *Paint It Today*, pp. 46, 48.
72   H.D., *Tribute to Freud*, p. 135.
73   H.D., *Asphodel*, p. 162.

4 'to make a self', 1919–26

1   Bryher, *Two Novels*, ed. Joanne Winning (Madison, WI, 2000), p. 289.
2   Bryher, *Heart to Artemis* (Ashfield, MA, 2006), p. 222.
3   H.D., *Paint It Today*, ed. Cassandra Laity (New York, 1992), p. 71.
4   Ibid.; H.D., *Asphodel*, p. 178.
5   H.D., *Paint It Today*, pp. 75, 81, 85.
6   Letter from H.D. to John Cournos dated [November 1919]; in 'Art and Ardor in World War One: Selected Letters from H.D. to John Cournos', ed. Donna Krolik Hollenberg, *Iowa Review*, XVI/3 (1986), pp. 126–55 (p. 146).
7   Susan McCabe, *H.D. and Bryher: An Untold Love Story of Modernism* (New York, 2021), p. 32.
8   Robert McAlmon and Kay Boyle, *Being Geniuses Together, 1920–1930* (San Francisco, CA, 1984), p. 2.
9   Bryher, *Two Novels*, p. 255.
10   Ibid., p. 24.
11   Ibid., p. 183.

12 Ibid., p. 164.

13 Ibid., p. 264.

14 Bryher, *Heart to Artemis*, p. 179.

15 Ibid., p. 183.

16 Ibid., p. 182.

17 Letter from H.D. to Bryher dated 20 April 1919. Bryher Papers, General Collection, Beinecke Rare Book and Manuscript Library, Yale University, New Haven, Connecticut.

18 H.D., *Tribute to Freud* (New York, 1984), p. 116.

19 H.D., *Notes on Thought and Vision* (London, 1988), pp. 18–19.

20 Ibid., pp. 22, 21.

21 H.D., *Tribute to Freud*, p. 130.

22 McCabe, *H.D. and Bryher*, p. 74.

23 Letter from Bryher to H.D. dated 9 June 1931. Bryher Papers.

24 H.D., *The Sword Went Out to Sea: Synthesis of a Dream, by Delia Alton*, ed. Cynthia Hogue and Julie Vandivere (Gainesville, FL, 2007), p. 203.

25 H.D., *Tribute to Freud*, p. 168.

26 Ibid., pp. 41, 45–6, 48.

27 Ibid., pp. 54–6 (emphasis in original).

28 Bryher, *Heart to Artemis*, p. 184.

29 Bryher, *West* (London, 1925), p. 57.

30 Ibid., p. 188.

31 Annette Debo, *The American H.D.* (Iowa City, IA, 2011), p. 4.

32 This point of disagreement persists well into the 1930s, but Havelock Ellis and Bryher discuss it early on in a letter dated 7 September 1919. Bryher Papers.

33 Perdita Schaffner, 'Running', *Iowa Review*, XVI/3 (1986), pp. 7–13 (p. 8).

34 Letter from H.D. to George Plank dated 7 November 1922[?]. George Plank Papers, Yale Collection of American Literature, Beinecke Rare Book and Manuscript Library, New Haven, Connecticut.

35 H.D., autobiographical notes. H.D. Papers, Yale Collection of American Literature, Beinecke Rare Book and Manuscript Library, New Haven, Connecticut.

36 Debo, *The American H.D.*, p. 42.

37 Bryher, 'Hellenics', *Poetry*, XVII/3 (1920), pp. 136–7.

38 H.D., *Collected Poems, 1912–1944*, ed. Louis L. Martz (New York, 1983), p. 272.

39 Ibid., p. 274.
40 Ibid., pp. 275, 277.
41 Alicia Ostriker, 'The Poet as Heroine: Learning to Read H.D.', *American Poetry Review*, XII/2 (1983), pp. 29–38 (p. 31).
42 Williams Carlos Williams, review of *Collected Poems of H.D.* H.D. Papers.
43 H.D., *Collected Poems*, pp. 134, 135.
44 Eileen Gregory, *H.D. and Hellenism: Classic Lines* (New York, 1997), p. 103.
45 H.D., *Collected Poems*, p. 133.
46 Ibid., p. 132.
47 Ostriker, 'The Poet as Heroine', p. 31.
48 H.D., *Collected Poems*, p. 109.
49 Letter from H.D. to Bryher dated [14 February 1919?]. Bryher Papers.
50 May Sinclair, 'The Poems of "H.D."', *Fortnightly Review*, CXXI/723 (March 1927), pp. 345, 344.
51 Marianne Moore, 'Hymen', *Broom*, IV/2 (January 1923), 133.
52 Letter from H.D. to Bryher dated [30 April 1924]. Bryher Papers.
53 Letter from H.D. to Bryher dated [18 September 1924]. Bryher Papers.
54 Letters from Bryher to H.D. dated [3 September 1924] and [1924?]. H.D. Papers.
55 Diana Collecott, *H.D. and Sapphic Modernism: 1910–1950* (New York, 1999), p. 206.
56 McCabe, *H.D. and Bryher*, p. 6.
57 Ibid., pp. 101–2.
58 Letter from Norman Douglas to Bryher dated 20 October 1921. Bryher Papers.
59 Rachel Hope Cleves, *Unspeakable: A Life beyond Sexual Morality* (Chicago, IL, 2020), p. 183.
60 Perdita Schaffner, 'Afterword: Profound Animal', in H.D., *Bid Me to Live (A Madrigal)*, ed. Caroline Zilboorg (Gainesville, FL, 2014), pp. 189, 191.
61 H.D., *Asphodel*, p. 94.
62 H.D., 'Tatter', *The European Caravan: An Anthology of the New Spirit in European Literature*, part 1 (New York, 1931), p. 485.
63 Letter from Frances Gregg to H.D. dated 20 November 1934. Silvia Dobson Papers, Beinecke Rare Book and Manuscript Library, Yale University, New Haven, Connecticut.

64 Letters from Brigit Patmore to H.D. dated 28 July 1924 and 30 July 1924. H.D. Papers.

65 Oliver Marlow Wilkinson, 'Frances Gregg: First Hand', in Frances Gregg, *The Mystic Leeway*, ed. Ben Jones (Ottawa, ON, 1995), p. 25.

66 Letter from Brigit Patmore to H.D. dated 31 January 1925. H.D. Papers.

67 Letter from Havelock Ellis to Bryher dated 16 August 1919. Bryher Papers.

68 Letter from H.D. to Bryher dated [22 April 1924]. Bryher Papers.

69 Letter from Bryher to H.D. dated [September 1924]. H.D. Papers

70 See McCabe, *H.D. and Bryher*, pp. 101–13.

71 Letter from Bryher to H.D. dated 14 June 1923. H.D. Papers.

72 Letter from Bryher to H.D. dated 18 June 1923. H.D. Papers

73 Schaffner, 'Running', p. 7.

74 Perdita Schaffner, 'Pandora's Box', in H.D., *HERmione* (New York, 1981), p. viii.

75 Susan Stanford Friedman, ed., *Analyzing Freud: Letters of H.D., Bryher, and Their Circle* (New York, 2002), p. xxxiii.

76 Schaffner, 'Pandora's Box', p. ix.

77 Schaffner, 'Running', p. 8.

78 Perdita Schaffner, 'Sketch of H.D.: The Egyptian Cat', in H.D., *Hedylus* (Redding Ridge, CT, 1980), p. 144.

79 Schaffner, 'Running', p. 7.

80 Ibid., p. 8.

81 Perdita Schaffner, untitled autobiographical manuscript. H.D. Papers.

82 H.D., *Paint It Today*, p. 5.

83 Schaffner, 'Pandora's Box', p. ix.

84 Schaffner, untitled autobiographical manuscript. H.D. Papers.

85 Schaffner, 'Pandora's Box', p. ix.

86 H.D., 'Notes on Euripides, Pausanius, and Greek Lyric Poets', H.D. Papers.

87 Steven Yao, *Translation and the Languages of Modernism: Gender, Politics, Language* (New York, 2002), p. 106.

88 H.D., *Collected Poems*, pp. 154–5.

89 Letter from H.D. to Glenn Hughes dated Tuesday, 1929. Glenn Hughes Collection, Harry Ransom Center, University of Texas at Austin.

90 Letter to Viola Baxter Jordan dated 29 March 1926[?]. Viola Baxter Jordan Papers, Beinecke Rare Book and Manuscript Library, Yale University, New Haven, Connecticut.

91 H.D., *Paint It Today*, p. 26.
92 H.D., 'H.D. by Delia Alton', *Iowa Review*, XVI/3 (1986), p. 220.
93 Letter from H.D. to H. P. Collins [1925?]. H.D. Papers.
94 Susan Stanford Friedman, *Penelope's Web* (New York, 1990), p. 251.
95 H.D., *Pilate's Wife*, ed. Joan Burke (New York, 2000), p. 49.
96 Joan Burke, 'Introduction', ibid., p. i.
97 H.D., *Magic Mirror, Compassionate Friendship, Thorn Thicket: A Tribute to Erich Heydt*, ed. Nephie J. Christodoulides (Victoria, BC, 2012), p. 98.
98 H.D., 'H.D. by Delia Alton', p. 230.
99 H.D., *Hedylus*, p. 78.
100 Ibid., p. 221.
101 H.D., *Collected Poems*, p. 352.

5 'the perfect bi-', 1927–39

1 Perdita Schaffner, 'Pandora's Box', in H.D., HERmione (New York, 1981), p. x.
2 William Bird, 'Impending Divorce of Poet Surprises', *Ogden Standard-Examiner* (12 June 1927), p. 7. This is the version I obtained, but it was a widely syndicated article throughout the United States.
3 Oliver Marlow Wilkinson, 'Frances Gregg: First Hand', in Frances Gregg, *The Mystic Leeway*, ed. Ben Jones (Ottawa, ON, 1995), p. 31.
4 H.D. [as John Helforth], *Nights* (New York, 1986), p. 46.
5 Perdita Schaffner, untitled autobiographical manuscript. H.D. Papers, Yale Collection of American Literature, Beinecke Rare Book and Manuscript Library, New Haven, Connecticut.
6 Letter from Kenneth Macpherson to H.D. [1928]. H.D. Papers.
7 Letter from Kenneth Macpherson to H.D. [1928]. H.D. Papers.
8 Letter from Bryher to Kenneth Macpherson [1928]. Bryher Papers, General Collection, Beinecke Rare Book and Manuscript Library, Yale University, New Haven, Connecticut.
9 Perdita Schaffner, 'Sketch of H.D.: The Egyptian Cat', in H.D., *Hedylus* (Redding Ridge, CT, 1980), p. 145.
10 'Confessions-Questionnaire', *The Little Review Anthology*, ed. Margaret Anderson (New York, 1970), p. 364.

11   H.D., *Collected Poems, 1912–1944*, ed. Louis L. Martz (New York, 1983), p. 349.

12   Ibid., p. 358.

13   Ibid., p. 353.

14   H.D., 'The Cinema and the Classics: Beauty', *Close Up*, I/1 (July 1927), p. 27.

15   Bryher, autobiographical notes. Bryher Papers.

16   James Donald, Anne Friedberg and Laura Marcus, 'Preface', in *Close Up, 1927–1933: Cinema and Modernism*, ed. James Donald, Anne Friedberg and Laura Marcus (Princeton, NJ, 1999), p. vii.

17   Anne Friedberg, 'Reading *Close Up*, 1927–1933', in *Close Up, 1927–1933*, ed. Donald, Friedberg and Marcus, pp. 1–29 (p. 3).

18   Betsy van Schlun, *The Pool Group and the Quest for Anthropological Universality: The Humane Image of Modernism* (Berlin, 2016), p. 362.

19   H.D., 'Joan of Arc', *Close Up*, III/1 (July 1928), p. 22.

20   H.D., 'An Appreciation', *Close Up*, IV/3 (March 1929), p. 59.

21   H.D., 'Russian Films', *Close Up*, III/3 (September 1928), p. 28.

22   H.D., 'The Cinema and the Classics: Beauty', p. 27.

23   Ibid., p. 26.

24   H.D., 'King of Kings Again' *Close Up*, II/2 (February 1928), p. 27 (emphasis in original).

25   H.D., 'An Appreciation', pp. 64–5, 61.

26   Letter from Kenneth Macpherson to H.D. [1928]. H.D. Papers.

27   Van Schlun, *The Pool Group*, p. 259.

28   Letter from H.D. to George Plank [dated 12 June 1928]. George Plank Papers, Yale Collection of American Literature, Beinecke Rare Book and Manuscript Library, New Haven, Connecticut.

29   Susan McCabe, *Cinematic Modernism: Modernist Poetry and Film* (New York, 2009), p. 167.

30   H.D., 'The Borderline Pamphlet', *Sagetrieb*, VI/2 (1987), p. 47.

31   'Confessions-Questionnaire', p. 364.

32   Letter from H.D. to Bryher [prob. 13 May 1930]. Bryher Papers.

33   Martin Bauml Duberman, *Paul Robeson: A Biography* (New York, 1988), p. 131.

34   Annette Debo, 'Interracial Modernism in Avant-Garde Film: Paul Robeson and H.D. in the 1930 *Borderline*', *Quarterly Review of Film and Video*, XVIII/4 (2001), pp. 371–83 (p. 380).

35 Eileen Gregory, *H.D. and Hellenism: Classic Lines* (New York, 1997), p. 181.

36 H.D., *Hippolytus Temporizes and Ion* (New York, 2003), p. 171.

37 Ibid., pp. 172–3.

38 Perdita Schaffner, 'Introduction', in H.D., *Nights*, p. xii.

39 Letter from Conrad Aiken to H.D. dated 31 October 1934. H.D. Papers.

40 Letter from Marianne Moore to H.D., in Annette Debo, *The American H.D.* (Iowa City, IA, 2011), p. 56.

41 Letter from H.D. to George Plank dated 16 October [1934]. George Plank Papers.

42 H.D., *The Usual Star* (Dijon, 1934), pp. 42, 69.

43 'Poetry Chiseled from Crystal with Care', *Dubuque Telegraph-Herald and Times-Journal* (6 March 1932), p. 5.

44 H.D., *Tribute to Freud* (New York, 1984), p. 13.

45 Perdita Schaffner, 'Running', *Iowa Review*, XVI/3 (1986), p. 10.

46 Letter from H.D. to Kenneth Macpherson dated [10? 1930?]. H.D. Papers.

47 Susan Stanford Friedman, *Psyche Reborn: The Emergence of H.D.* (Bloomington, IN, 1987), p. 17.

48 H.D., *Hirslanden Notebooks*, ed. Matte Robinson and Demetres P. Tryphonopoulos (Victoria, BC, 2012), p. 16.

49 H.D., *Tribute to Freud*, p. 16 (emphasis in original).

50 Ibid., p. 69.

51 Letter from H.D. to Bryher dated 26 May [1933], in Friedman, *Analyzing Freud*, p. 325.

52 Letter from H.D. to Bryher dated 18 March [1933], in Friedman, *Analyzing Freud*, p. 112.

53 Letter from H.D. to Bryher dated 17 March [1933], in Friedman, *Analyzing Freud*, p. 107.

54 Letter from H.D. to Bryher and Kenneth Macpherson dated [23 March 1933], in Friedman, *Analyzing Freud*, p. 140.

55 Letter from H.D. to Bryher dated 2 May [1933], in Friedman, *Analyzing Freud*, p. 232.

56 Letter from H.D. to Bryher dated 3 May [1933], in Friedman, *Analyzing Freud*, p. 235.

57 Letter from H.D. to Bryher dated 17 May [1933], in Friedman, *Analyzing Freud*, p. 287.

58   Letter from H.D. to Bryher dated 15 March [1933], in Friedman, *Analyzing Freud*, p. 96.

59   Letter from H.D. to Bryher dated 22 March [1933], in Friedman, *Analyzing Freud*, p. 136.

60   Letter from H.D. to Bryher dated 26 March [1933], in Friedman, *Analyzing Freud*, p. 199.

61   Donna Krolik Hollenberg, *Winged Words: The Life and Work of the Poet H.D.* (Ann Arbor, MI, 2022), p. 161.

62   H.D., *Tribute to Freud*, p. 58.

63   Ibid., p. 59.

64   Ibid., p. 152.

65   See Friedman, *Psyche Reborn*.

66   Letter from H.D. to Bryher dated 24 November [1934], in Friedman, *Analyzing Freud*, p. 497.

67   Letter from H.D. to Bryher dated 2 May [1936], in Friedman, *Analyzing Freud*, p. xxxiv.

68   Letter from H.D. to Bryher dated 24 November [1934], in Friedman, *Analyzing Freud*, p. 498.

69   Friedman, *Analyzing Freud*, p. xvii.

70   H.D., *Collected Poems*, p. 451.

71   Ibid., p. 453.

72   Ibid., p. 455.

73   Letter from H.D. to Bryher dated 18 May [1933], in Friedman, *Analyzing Freud*, p. 291.

74   Letter from H.D. to Bryher dated 15 May [1933]. Bryher Papers.

75   Letter from H.D. to Bryher dated 16 December [1934], in Friedman, *Analyzing Freud*, p. 521.

76   Letter from H.D. to Bryher dated 14 August [1935]. Bryher Papers.

77   Letter from Sigmund Freud to H.D. dated 26 February [1937], in Friedman, *Analyzing Freud*, p. 534.

78   Letter from Richard Aldington to H.D. dated 15 January 1937. H.D. Papers.

79   H.D., divorce papers. H.D. Papers.

80   Letter from H.D. to George Plank [27 April 1935]. George Plank Papers.

81   Letter from H.D. to George Plank [19 July 1938]. George Plank Papers.

82   Lara Vetter, *A Curious Peril: H.D.'s Late Modernist Prose* (Gainesville, FL, 2017), p. 14.

6 'this is not writing, this is burning', 1939–46

1   Letter from H.D. to Bryher dated 11 November [1939]. Bryher Papers, General Collection, Beinecke Rare Book and Manuscript Library, Yale University, New Haven, Connecticut.
2   Letter from Bryher to H.D. dated 6 March 1940. H.D. Papers, Yale Collection of American Literature, Beinecke Rare Book and Manuscript Library, New Haven, Connecticut.
3   Letter from H.D. to Bryher dated 3 June [1940]. Bryher Papers.
4   Letter from H.D. to May Sarton dated 19 June [1940]. May Sarton Papers. The Henry W. and Albert A. Berg Collection of English and American Literature, New York Public Library, Astor, Lenox and Tilden Foundations, New York.
5   Letter from Robert Herring to H.D. dated 20 June 1940. H.D. Papers.
6   Letter from Kenneth Macpherson to H.D. dated [1940?]. H.D. Papers
7   Letter from H.D. to Doris Long dated [194?]. H.D. Papers.
8   Letter from H.D. to George Plank dated [7 January 1941]. George Plank Papers, Yale Collection of American Literature, Beinecke Rare Book and Manuscript Library, New Haven, Connecticut.
9   Letter from H.D. to Marianne Moore dated 24 September 1940. Louis Silverstein, 'H.D. Chronology, Part Four', available at www.imagists.org, accessed 28 July 2022.
10 Letter from H.D. to Bryher dated 19 June [1940]. Bryher Papers.
11 Bryher, *The Days of Mars: A Memoir, 1940–1946* (New York, 1972), p. 4.
12 Perdita Schaffner, 'Unless a Bomb Falls', in H.D., *The Gift* (New York, 1982), p. xxi.
13 Bryher, *The Days of Mars*, pp. 13–14.
14 Perdita Schaffner, unpublished memoir. H.D. Papers.
15 Letter from H.D. to Viola Baxter Jordan dated [30 July 1944]. Viola Baxter Jordan Papers, Beinecke Rare Book and Manuscript Library, Yale University, New Haven, Connecticut. This letter is misdated; it is from 1941.
16 Bryher, *The Days of Mars*, p. 31.
17 H.D., *The Gift*, ed. Jane Augustine (Gainesville, FL, 1998), p. 109.
18 Letter from H.D. to May Sarton dated 5 February [1941?]. May Sarton Papers.

19   Annette Debo, 'Introduction', in H.D., *Within the Walls and What Do I Love?*, ed. Annette Debo (Gainesville, FL, 2014), p. 16.

20   Schaffner, 'Unless a Bomb Falls', p. xxi.

21   Letter from H.D. to Molly Hughes dated 14 November 1943. H.D. Papers

22   On food and rationing during the war, see Annette Debo, *The American H.D.* (Iowa City, IA, 2011), p. 134.

23   Perdita Schaffner, untitled autobiographical manuscript. H.D. Papers.

24   Bryher, autobiographical notes. Bryher papers.

25   H.D., 'A Letter from England', *Bryn Mawr Alumnae Bulletin*, XXI/7 (1941), p. 22.

26   Letter from H.D. to May Sarton dated 5 February [1941]. May Sarton Papers.

27   H.D., *Within the Walls*, p. 160.

28   Letter from H.D. to Viola Baxter Jordan dated 10 November [1941]. Viola Baxter Jordan Papers, Beinecke Rare Book and Manuscript Library, Yale University, New Haven, Connecticut.

29   Perdita Schaffner, unpublished memoir. H.D. Papers.

30   Bryher, autobiographical notes. Bryher Papers.

31   Letter from H.D. to Clifford Howard dated 26 September [1940]. H.D. Papers.

32   H.D., 'A Letter from England', pp. 22–3.

33   Letter from H.D. to Bryher dated 11 December [1941]. Bryher Papers.

34   H.D., *The Gift*, pp. 109–10.

35   Schaffner, 'Unless a Bomb Falls', p. xxi.

36   H.D., *The Gift*, p. 218.

37   Bryher, *The Days of Mars*, p. xi.

38   Ibid., p. ix.

39   Letter from H.D. to Francis Wolle dated 13 January [1946]. H.D. Papers.

40   Letter from H.D. to May Sarton dated 6 December [1944]. May Sarton Papers.

41   Bryher, autobiographical notes. Bryher Papers.

42   H.D., *Within the Walls*, p. 123.

43   Bryher, *The Days of Mars*, p. 111.

44   Letter from H.D. to Clifford Howard dated 9 November [1941]. H.D. Papers.

45   Francis Wolle, *A Moravian Heritage* (Boulder, CO, 1972), p. 128.

46   Letter from H.D. to Viola Baxter Jordan dated 28 July [1942]. Viola
     Baxter Jordan Papers.
47   Letter from H.D. to May Sarton dated 13 October [1941]. May Sarton
     Papers.
48   Letter from H.D. to Viola Baxter Jordan dated 15 February [1945].
     Viola Baxter Jordan Papers.
49   Letter from H.D. to Bryher dated 16 May [1939]. Bryher Papers.
50   Letter from H.D. to Clifford Howard dated 9 November [1941]. H.D. Papers.
51   H.D., *The Gift*, p. 111.
52   H.D., *Within the Walls*, p. 113.
53   Letter from H.D. to May Sarton dated 29 July [1942]. May Sarton
     Papers.
54   Peter Thorsheim, *Waste into Weapons: Recycling in Britain during the
     Second World War* (New York, 2015), p. 2.
55   H.D., *Trilogy*, ed. Aliki Barnstone (New York, 1998), p. 16.
56   Letters from H.D. to May Sarton dated 29 July [1942] and 4 June
     [1944]. May Sarton Papers.
57   Letter from H.D. to May Sarton dated 15 October [1943]. May Sarton
     Papers.
58   H.D., *The Gift*, pp. 121–2.
59   Ibid., p. 109.
60   H.D., *Within the Walls*, p. 121.
61   H.D., 'H.D. by Delia Alton', *Iowa Review*, XVI/3 (1986), p. 186.
62   Robert Duncan, *The H.D. Book*, ed. Michael Boughn and Victor
     Coleman (Berkeley, CA, 2011), p. 298.
63   Letter from H.D. to May Sarton dated 24 January 24 [1942].
     May Sarton Papers.
64   Letter from H.D. to Viola Baxter Jordan dated [30 July 1944].
     Viola Baxter Jordan Papers. This letter is misdated; it is from 1941.
65   H.D., *Trilogy*, p. 3.
66   Letter from H.D. to Molly Hughes dated 6 May [1942]. H.D. Papers.
67   Letter from H.D. to Molly Hughes dated 5 August [1942]. H.D. Papers.
68   H.D., *Trilogy*, p. 5.
69   Ibid., p. 14.
70   Ibid., p. 9.
71   Ibid., p. 4.
72   Ibid., p. 12.

73 Letter from H.D. to Doris Long dated 4 June [1944]. H.D. Papers.
74 Letter from Vita Sackville-West to H.D. dated 5 June 1944. H.D. Papers.
75 Letter from H.D. to May Sarton dated 13 July [1944]. May Sarton
     Papers.
76 H.D., *Trilogy*, p. 59 (italics in original).
77 Ibid., p. 123.
78 Ibid., pp. 74–5.
79 Ibid., p. 16.
80 Ibid., p. 129.
81 Letter from H.D. to Silvia Dobson dated 4 August [1944]. Silvia
     Dobson Papers, Beinecke Rare Book and Manuscript Library, Yale
     University, New Haven, Connecticut.
82 Letter from H.D. to May Sarton dated 25 August [1944]. May Sarton
     Papers.
83 Bryher, *The Days of Mars*, p. 151.
84 H.D., *Within the Walls*, p. 173.
85 Letter from H.D. to Gretchen Baker dated 2 August [1945].
     H.D. Papers.
86 Letter from H.D. to Viola Baxter Jordan dated 18 May [1945]. Viola
     Baxter Jordan Papers.

7 'content, besieged with memories, like low-swarming bees',
1946–61

1 Jane Augustine, 'Introduction', in H.D., *The Mystery*, ed. Jane
    Augustine (Gainesville, FL, 2009), pp. 127, 167, 180–81. See also Lara
    Vetter, *A Curious Peril: H.D.'s Late Modernist Prose* (Gainesville, FL,
    2017), p. 75.
2 H.D., *By Avon River*, ed. Lara Vetter (Gainesville, FL, 2014), p. 61.
3 Ibid., p. 75.
4 Letter from H.D. to George Plank dated 9 July [1949]. George Plank
    Papers, Yale Collection of American Literature, Beinecke Rare Book
    and Manuscript Library, New Haven, Connecticut.
5 Letter from H.D. to Bryher dated 17 August [1949]. Bryher Papers,
    General Collection, Beinecke Rare Book and Manuscript Library, Yale
    University, New Haven, Connecticut.

6   Letter from H.D. to Norman Holmes Pearson dated 14 June [1950].
    Norman Holmes Pearson Papers, Yale Collection of American Literature,
    Beinecke Rare Book and Manuscript Library, New Haven, Connecticut.

7   Letter from H.D. to Norman Holmes Pearson dated 31 July [1948],
    in *Between History and Poetry: The Letters of H.D. and Norman Holmes
    Pearson*, ed. Donna Krolik Hollenberg (Iowa City, IA, 1997), p. 76.

8   H.D., 'H.D. by Delia Alton', *Iowa Review*, XVI/3 (1986), pp. 186, 193.

9   Letter from H.D. to Norman Holmes Pearson dated 4 October [1951].
    Norman Holmes Pearson Papers.

10 Letter from H.D. to Bryher dated 18 November 1948. Bryher Papers.

11 Oliver Marlow Wilkinson, 'Frances Gregg: First Hand', in Frances
    Gregg, *The Mystic Leeway*, ed. Ben Jones (Ottawa, ON, 1995), pp. 19–20.

12 Donna Krolik Hollenberg, *Winged Words: The Life and Work of the Poet
    H.D.* (Ann Arbor, MI, 2022), p. 218.

13 Letter from Perdita Schaffner to H.D. dated 4 April 1947. H.D. Papers,
    Yale Collection of American Literature, Beinecke Rare Book and
    Manuscript Library, New Haven, Connecticut.

14 Letter from H.D. to Richard Aldington dated 1 July [1950]. H.D. Papers.

15 Letter from Perdita Schaffner to H.D. dated 10 May 1950. H.D. Papers

16 H.D., *Magic Mirror, Compassionate Friendship, Thorn Thicket: A Tribute
    to Erich Heydt*, ed. Nephie J. Christodoulides (Victoria, BC, 2012), p. 136.

17 H.D., *Magic Mirror*, p. 94.

18 Elizabeth Willis, 'A Public History of the Dividing Line: H.D., the
    Bomb, and the Roots of the Postmodern', *Arizona Quarterly*, LXIII/1
    (2007), pp. 81–108 (p. 101).

19 Letters from H.D. to Bryher dated 10, 11 and 14 October [1952]. Bryher
    Papers.

20 Albert Gelpi, 'Hilda in Egypt', *Southern Review*, XVIII/2 (1982), p. 233.

21 Matte Robinson, *The Astral H.D.: Occult and Religious Sources and
    Contexts for H.D.'s Poetry and Prose* (New York, 2016), p. 31.

22 H.D., *Helen in Egypt* (New York, 1961), p. 17.

23 Ibid., pp. 22, 23.

24 Ibid., p. 187.

25 Ibid., p. 232.

26 Cynthia Hogue, 'On Being "Ill"-Informed: H.D.'s Late Modernist
    Poetics (of) *d'espère*', *Jacket2* (9 July 2018), available at https://
    jacket2.org.

27 H.D., *Magic Mirror*, p. 91.

28 Ibid., p. 94.

29 Letter from Erich Heydt to Barbara Guest dated 20 July 1982. Barbara Guest Papers, Beinecke Rare Book and Manuscript Library, Yale University, New Haven, Connecticut.

30 Matte Robinson, Introduction, in H.D., *Hirslanden Notebooks*, ed. Matte Robinson and Demetres P. Tryphonopoulos (Victoria, BC, 2012), p. xii.

31 H.D., *Hirslanden Notebooks*, p. 39.

32 Ibid., p. 11.

33 Robert Duncan, *The H.D. Book*, ed. Michael Boughn and Victor Coleman (Berkeley, CA, 2011), p. 422.

34 Perdita Schaffner, 'Running', *Iowa Review*, XVI/3 (1986), p. 12. Letter from Perdita Schaffner to Norman Holmes Pearson dated 28 May 1959. Norman Holmes Pearson Papers.

35 H.D., *End to Torment* (New York, 1979), p. 19.

36 Letter to Viola Baxter Jordan dated July 5, 1942. Viola Baxter Jordan Papers, Beinecke Rare Book and Manuscript Library, Yale University, New Haven, Connecticut.

37 Letter from H.D. to Richard Aldington dated 1 November [1951]. H.D. Papers.

38 Letter from Robert Duncan to Denise Levertov dated 19 April 1961, in *The Letters of Robert Duncan and Denise Levertov*, ed. Robert J. Bertholf and Albert Gelpi (Stanford, CA, 2003), p. 289.

39 H.D., *Magic Mirror*, p. 174. This claim is implicit in the title of Matte Robinson's book, *The Astral H.D.*

40 The term is from Rachel Blau DuPlessis, 'Romantic Thralldom in H.D.', *Contemporary Literature*, XX/2 (1979), pp. 178–203.

41 H.D., *Hermetic Definition*, p. 11.

42 Ibid., p. 14.

43 Letter from H.D. to Richard Aldington dated 27 April [1957]. H.D. Papers.

44 H.D., *Hermetic Definition*, p. 81.

45 Ibid., p. 3.

46 Raffaella Baccolini, '"There Was a Helen before There Was a War": Memory and Desire in H.D.'s *Winter Love* and Pound's *Pisan Cantos*', *Sagetrieb*, XV/1/2 (1996), p. 237.

47 Lionel Durand, 'Life in a Hothouse', *Newsweek*, LV (2 May 1960), p. 92.

48 H.D., *Hermetic Definition*, pp. 7, 20.

49 Ibid., p. 49.

50 Ibid., p. 55.

51 Hogue, 'On Being "Ill"-Informed'.

52 Kathleen Crown, '"Let Us Endure": Atomic-Age Anxiety in H.D.'s *Sagesse*', *Sagetrieb*, XV (1996), p. 268.

53 Schaffner, 'Running', p. 12.

54 Harriet Stix, 'Prize-Winning "H.D." Is Returning Native', *NY Herald Tribune* (25 May 1960), p. 21.

55 Duncan, *The H.D. Book*, p. 183.

56 Ibid., p. 217.

57 Durand, 'Life in a Hothouse', p. 93.

58 Letter from H.D. to Richard Aldington dated 23 April [1959]. H.D. Papers.

59 Durand, 'Life in a Hothouse', p. 92.

60 Letters from Erich Heydt to Barbara Guest dated 24 August 1982 and 20 July 1982. Barbara Guest Papers.

61 H.D., *Hirslanden Notebooks*, pp. 64–5.

62 Letter from Robert Duncan to Denise Levertov dated 14 July 1961, in *The Letters of Robert Duncan and Denise Levertov*, p. 296.

63 Denise Levertov, *The Collected Poems of Denise Levertov* (New York, 2013), p. 188.

64 Robert Duncan, *Roots and Branches* (New York, 1964), p. 88.

65 Letter from Robert Duncan to Denise Levertov dated 15 September 1961, in *The Letters of Robert Duncan and Denise Levertov*, p. 309.

66 H.D., *Collected Poems, 1912–1944*, ed. Louis L. Martz (New York, 1983), pp. 299–300.

Select Bibliography

Selected works by H.D.

Asphodel, ed. Robert Spoo (Durham, NC, 1992)

Bid Me to Live (A Madrigal), ed. Caroline Zilboorg (Gainesville, FL, 2011)

Borderline, in *Paul Robeson: Portraits of the Artist* (Criterion Collection, 2007)

'The Borderline Pamphlet', *Sagetrieb*, VI/2 (1987)

By Avon River, ed. Lara Vetter (Gainesville, FL, 2014)

Choruses from the Iphigeneia in Aulis and the Hippolytus of Euripides (London, 1919)

Close Up film reviews and criticism:

    'An Appreciation', III/3 (March 1929)

    'Boo (Sirocco and the Screen)', II/1 (January 1928)

    'The Cinema and the Classics: Beauty', I/1 (July 1927)

    'The Cinema and the Classics: The Mask and the Movietone', I/5 (November 1927)

    'The Cinema and the Classics: Restraint', I/2 (August 1927)

    'Conrad Veidt: The Student of Prague', I/3 (September 1927)

    'Expiation', II/5 (May 1928)

    'Joan of Arc', II/7 (July 1928)

    'King of Kings Again', II/2 (February 1928)

    'Russian Films', II/9 (September 1928)

    'Turksrib', III/12 (December 1929)

Collected Poems, 1912–1944 [1986], ed. Louis L. Martz (Manchester, 1996)

End to Torment [1979], ed. Norman Holmes Pearson and Michael King (Manchester, 1980)

The Gift, ed. Jane Augustine (Gainesville, FL, 1998)

The Hedgehog (New York, 1988)

Hedylus, ed. Perdita Schaffner (Manchester, 1980)

Helen in Egypt [1961] (Manchester, 1985); excerpts of H.D. reading from
     drafts of this poem can be found at PennSound, https://writing.
     upenn.edu/pennsound
Hermetic Definition [1972], ed. Norman Holmes Pearson (Manchester, 2017)
HERmione (New York, 1981)
Hippolytus Temporizes and Ion (New York, 2003)
Hirslanden Notebooks, ed. Matte Robinson and Demetres P.
     Tryphonopoulos (Victoria, BC, 2015)
Kora and Ka (New York, 1996)
Magic Mirror, Compassionate Friendship, Thorn Thicket, ed. Nephie J.
     Christodoulides (Victoria, BC, 2012)
Majic Ring, ed. Demetres P. Tryphonopoulos (Gainesville, FL, 2009)
The Mystery, ed. Jane Augustine (Gainesville, FL, 2009)
Narthex and Other Stories, ed Michael Boughn (Toronto, ON, 2013)
Nights (New York, 1986)
Notes on Thought and Vision (London, 1982)
Paint It Today, ed. Cassandra Laity (New York, 1992)
Palimpsest (Carbondale, IL, 1968)
Pilate's Wife, ed. Joan A. Burke (New York, 2000)
Selected Poems, ed. Louis Martz (Manchester, 1997)
'The Suffragette', ed. Donna Krolik Hollenberg, *Sagetrieb*, XV/1–2 (1996)
The Sword Went Out to Sea: Synthesis of a Dream, by Delia Alton, ed. Cynthia
     Hogue and Julie Vandivere (Gainesville, FL, 2007)
Tribute to Freud [1984], ed. Norman Holmes Pearson (Manchester, 1997)
Trilogy, ed. Aliki Barnstone [1998], ed. Norman Holmes Pearson
     (Manchester, 1997)
The Usual Star (Dijon, 1934)
Vale Ave (New York, 2013)
White Rose and the Red, ed. Alison Halsall (Gainesville, FL, 2009)
Within the Walls and What Do I Love?, ed. Annette Debo (Gainesville, FL, 2014)

Selected Works about H.D.

Anderson, Elizabeth, *H.D. and Modernist Religious Imagination: Mysticism
     and Writing* (New York, 2013)
Baccolini, Raffaella, *Tradition, Identity, Desire: Revisionist Strategies in H.D.'s
     Late Poetry* (Bologna, 1995)

Boughn, Michael, *H.D.: A Bibliography, 1905–1990* (Charlottesville, VA, 1993)

Bryant, Marsha, and Mary Ann Eaverly, 'Egypto-Modernism: James Henry Breasted, H.D., and the New Past', *Modernism/Modernity*, XIV/3 (2007), pp. 435–53

Collecott, Diana, *H.D. and Sapphic Modernism, 1910–1950* (New York, 1999)

Connor, Rachel, *H.D. and the Image* (Manchester, 2004)

Debo, Annette, *The American H.D.* (Iowa City, IA, 2012)

Detloff, Madelyn, 'H.D.'s Wars', in *The Persistence of Modernism: Loss and Mourning in the Twentieth Century* (New York, 2009)

Duncan, Robert, *The H.D. Book*, ed. Michael Boughn and Victor Coleman (Berkeley, CA, 2011)

DuPlessis, Rachel Blau, 'Romantic Thralldom in H.D.', *Contemporary Literature*, XX/2 (1979), pp. 178–203

Emerson, Kent, 'H.D.'s Interfaces', *Modernism/Modernity Print+*, IV/4 (2020), available at https://modernismmodernity.org

Friedman, Susan Stanford, *Penelope's Web: Gender, Modernity, H.D.'s Fiction* (New York, 1990)

—, *Psyche Reborn: The Emergence of H.D.* (Bloomington, IN, 1981)

—, 'Who Buried H.D.? A Poet, Her Critics, and Her Place in "The Literary Tradition"', *College English*, XXXVI/7 (1975), pp. 801–14

—, ed., *Analyzing Freud: Letters of H.D., Bryher, and Their Circle* (New York, 2002)

—, and Rachel Blau DuPlessis, eds, *Signets: Reading H.D.* (Madison, WI, 1990)

Graham, Sarah H. S., '"We Have a Secret. We Are Alive": H.D.'s *Trilogy* as a Response to War', *Texas Studies in Literature and Language*, XLIV/2 (2002), pp. 161–210

Gregg, Frances, *The Mystic Leeway*, ed. Ben Jones (Ottawa, ON, 1995)

Gregory, Eileen, *H.D. and Hellenism: Classic Lines*, (New York, 1997)

Gubar, Susan, 'The Echoing Spell of H.D.'s *Trilogy*', *Contemporary Literature*, XIX/2 (1978), pp. 196–218

Hanscombe, Gillian, and Virginia L. Smyers, *Writing for Their Lives: The Modernist Women, 1910–1940* (London, 1987)

Hatlen, Burton, 'The Imagist Poetics of H.D.'s *Sea Garden*', *Paideuma*, XXIV/2–3 (1995), pp. 107–30

H.D. Papers, Yale Collection of American Literature, Beinecke Rare Book and Manuscript Library (New Haven, CT)

Hickman, Miranda, and Lynn Kozak, eds, *The Classics in Modernist Translation* (New York, 2019)

Hogue, Cynthia, 'On Being "Ill"-Informed: H.D.'s Late Modernist Poetics
   (of) *d'espère*', *Jacket2* (9 July 2018) available at https://jacket2.org
Hollenberg, Donna Krolik, *Winged Words: The Life and Work of the Poet H.D.*
   (Ann Arbor, MI, 2022)
—, ed., *Between History and Poetry: The Letters of H.D. and Norman Holmes
   Pearson* (Iowa City, IA, 1997)
—, ed., *H.D. and Poets After* (Iowa City, IA, 2000)
King, Michael, ed., *H.D.: Woman and Poet* (Orono, ME, 1986)
Laity, Cassandra, *H.D. and the Victorian Fin de Siècle: Gender, Modernism,
   Decadence* (New York, 1996)
McCabe, Susan, *H.D. and Bryher: An Untold Love Story of Modernism* (New
   York, 2021)
Morris, Adalaide, *How to Live/What to Do: H.D.'s Cultural Poetics* (Urbana,
   IL, 2003)
Ostriker, Alicia, 'No Rule of Procedure: The Open Poetics of H.D.', *Agenda*,
   XXV/3–4 (1987), pp. 145–54
Pondrom, Cyrena N., 'H.D. and the Origins of Imagism', *Sagetrieb*, IV/1
   (1985), pp. 73–97
Rado, Lisa, '"The Perfection of the Fiery Moment": H.D. and the
   Androgynous Poetics of Overmind', in *The Modern Androgyne
   Imagination* (Charlottesville, VA, 2000), pp. 60–98
Robinson, Matte, *The Astral H.D.: Occult and Religious Sources and Contexts
   for H.D.'s Poetry and Prose* (New York, 2016)
Silverstein, Louis, 'H.D. Chronology', available at www.imagists.org
Taylor, Georgina, *H.D. and the Public Sphere of Modernist Women Writers,
   1913–1946: Talking Women* (New York, 2001)
Vetter, Lara, *A Curious Peril: H.D.'s Late Modernist Prose* (Gainesville, FL,
   2017)
Wade, Francesca, *Square Haunting: Five Writers in London between the Wars*
   (New York, 2021)
Walsh, Rebecca, 'H.D.'s *Trilogy* as Transnational Palimpsest', in *The
   Geopoetics of Modernism* (Gainesville, FL, 2015), pp. 124–46
Willis, Elizabeth, 'A Public History of the Dividing Line: H.D., the Bomb,
   and the Roots of the Postmodern', *Arizona Quarterly*, LXIII/1 (2007),
   pp. 81–108
Zilboorg, Caroline, ed., *Richard Aldington and H.D.: Their Lives in Letters*
   (Manchester, 2003)

Acknowledgements

What a joy to write a biographical study of an author I have spent so many years reading and admiring! My first debt of thanks, always, is to the extraordinarily generous community of H.D. scholars whom it's been such a privilege to know and from whom I've learned (and am still learning) so much. This book was written largely during the strange isolation of the COVID-19 pandemic – a truly solitary experience – but I have, inevitably and happily, drawn on decades of scholarship and conversations with others who share my fascination with H.D., most notably Annette Debo, who has been my partner in H.D. studies for half of my life now.

I would have never imagined myself a biographer before undertaking this project. I am ever grateful to Reaktion Books for giving me this opportunity, and to my editors – especially Vivian Constantinopoulos, who commissioned this book, and Amy Salter – for their expert stewardship of this project from its inception to its completion. Their sage advice and careful attention, at every step, has been essential to the project. Profuse thanks to both Mark Hall and Sophie Yates, who read parts of the manuscript and offered invaluable feedback.

I also benefited greatly from assistance from Nancy Kuhl and the outstanding staff of librarians at the Beinecke Rare Book and Manuscript Library at Yale University, where H.D.'s papers are held. Nancy was always eager to help with what must have felt like a barrage of research queries, even while the library remained closed through the pandemic. Elizabeth Garver, at the Harry Ransom Center of the University of Texas, graciously combed through dusty boxes to unearth a photograph of Frances Gregg.

On a personal note, I want to acknowledge my debt to Randy Malamud, who introduced me to H.D.'s writings in a course that was to set my research trajectory for decades to come. My gratitude to my father, Fred Vetter, who champions whatever and all ventures I undertake. Finally, my thanks to Kirk Melnikoff, for his love and unwavering encouragement through yet another project on H.D.

This project would have not been possible without the extraordinary generosity of H.D.'s family. For permission to quote from the unpublished writings of H.D., Bryher and Perdita Schaffner, I would like to thank Declan Spring and the Schaffner Family Foundation: Copyright © 2022 by The Schaffner Family Foundation. Used by permission. Published works by H.D. are used by permission of New Directions Publishing Corporation and Carcanet Press, Ltd.

Photo Acknowledgements

The author and publishers wish to express their thanks to the below sources of illustrative material and/or permission to reproduce it:

Beinecke Rare Book and Manuscript Library, courtesy of The Schaffner Family Foundation: pp. 6, 19, 22, 23, 25, 28, 29, 30, 57, 65, 67, 74, 78, 83, 86, 96, 102, 105, 109, 114, 116, 118, 121, 124, 153, 163, 167, 169, 173, 174; Harry Ransom Center, The University of Texas at Austin: p. 35; © Man Ray 2015 Trust / Artists Rights Society (ARS), NY/ADAGP, Paris 2022: p. 88.